Don't Quit Your Day Job!

Don't Quit Your Day Job!

WHAT YOU NEED TO KNOW
BEFORE YOU GO INTO BUSINESS
SO YOU CAN STAY IN BUSINESS

LARRY WINGET

MEDIA

Published 2021 by Gildan Media LLC
aka G&D Media
www.GandDmedia.com

Front cover design by David Rheinhardt of Pyrographx

Interior design by Meghan Day Healey of Story Horse, LLC

Library of Congress Cataloging-in-Publication Data is available upon request

ISBN: 978-1-7225-0511-0

10   9   8   7   6   5   4   3   2   1

Contents

Foreword

In this book, Larry Winget, the man they call the "Pitbull of Personal Development®," will tell you the truth about entrepreneurship and how to be a successful entrepreneur. True to form, what Larry has to tell you is quite a bit different from the traditional wisdom that you may have heard up until now.

According to Larry, the world is full of podcast speakers, so-called thought leaders, hustlers, and shysters, telling people to become entrepreneurs to attain financial freedom and achieve their dreams. These people promise grand results from proven methods. They say that if you find your passion and follow your dream, you'll live a life of love and luxury.

That's all baloney. According to the U.S. Bureau of Labor Statistics, 20 percent of new businesses fail during the first two years of being open, 45 percent during the first five years, and 65 percent during the first ten years. Is failure your dream? Is it your dream to lose your life savings and crush your family's future? If that's your idea of happiness, then quit your day job. Follow your dream and get ready to cry yourself to sleep at night.

As Larry says, people have been sold that old bag of hooey about what it takes to be successful. Passion is not it. Motivation is not it. Loving what you do is not it. Those things matter, of course, but barely. What matters is finding a problem and solving it; serving your customer better than your competition does; hiring and firing; managing your time, your resources, and your employees; knowing how to sell; knowing your numbers; and knowing what to do when it all goes to hell, because that is the only guarantee that there really is when starting your own business.

Just who is Larry Winget, and why is he qualified to advise you about starting your own business? Larry is quite an accomplished businessperson himself. He is a bestselling author, television personality, social commentator, and internationally acclaimed speaker. He has hosted his own television series on A&E, been featured in two CNBC specials, had his own PBS special, and is a regular contributor as a business guru on Fox News, Fox Business, and others news networks. He has also written six *New York Times* and *Wall Street Journal* bestsellers that have been translated into over twenty languages, including *It's Called Work for a Reason.*

Larry is also the author of seven bestselling audio programs such as the Politically Incorrect Success System. He's a member of the International Speakers Hall of Fame and has spoken to over 400 of the Fortune 500 companies. He was recently named one of the Top 50 Keynote Speakers In the World. Larry is known worldwide for being direct, caustic, irreverent, and in-your-face. He offers solid advice for improving your life, business, finances, and family. Not often will you find someone who can deliver solid information in such a humorous, thought-provoking, and transformational style.

In this book, you'll learn that Larry is not against starting your own business or becoming an entrepreneur. He is against doing it the wrong way: with no plan, little preparation, and only your passion to rely on. Dreams don't come true. Plans come true.

Larry will give you a plan to prepare yourself for the harsh reality of running your own business so you can be profitable—which is why you started your business in the first place.

1

Is Your Dream Really A Nightmare?

I'm a big believer in entrepreneurship. I believe it is the backbone of the entire financial structure of this country. We have to have entrepreneurship to keep our economy alive and thriving. However, most people who become entrepreneurs really should keep their day jobs. They need someone else to make sure the paycheck shows up on Friday. They are not responsible enough or prepared enough, they haven't done their homework, they haven't done the market analysis, and they have no business ever going into business; they need to leave it to someone else.

However, there is a small group that definitely ought to go out on their own, start their own businesses, start hiring people, create new products and services, deliver high-quality service to consumers, and make a great living doing it. But those people are in a minority.

Not Dirt-Poor, but Dusty

Let me step back in time for you and discuss my own career journey, both as an employee and an entrepreneur. I grew up, maybe not dirt-poor, but at least dusty, in Muskogee, Oklahoma. I watched my mom and dad go to work every single day for many years. My dad worked for Sears for forty-seven years. My mom worked at a little retail store next door to the Sears store in Muskogee. I was used to the fact that every single day you get up, you get dressed, and you go to work. Then you come home, and you still work, because there's a lot to do around the place. I was used to seeing people work at a job for a living. That was just part of the way I was raised, and I observed that that was how it was done in my family and in all the folks I grew up around.

I did see people starting their own businesses from time to time. I saw lots of little stores and operations pop up throughout Muskogee over the years, and I thought it was interesting to see new places to eat and shop but I also noticed that a lot of them went out of business.

I realized early on in my life that there was one thing I could bring to the marketplace that most people weren't doing (probably because they hadn't been taught), and that was willingness to do whatever it takes. I was willing to work, no matter how hard the work was or how much of it there was. I was used to seeing people work. I knew that when you worked hard, you were rewarded for it. It was a very simple concept: work hard, get paid. I understood that.

I asked my dad one time why he had been with Sears for forty-seven years. That was over twelve thousand days and I watched him go to work most of those days.

My dad said, "Larry, it's really very simple. When I went to work for Sears, I made them a deal: as long as you show up with the money, I'll show up with the work." And for forty-seven years, every other Friday, Sears was there with the money, which, to my dad, meant that he had to show up with the work. It was a deal that he made. To him, a deal was a deal. It wasn't based on motivation; it wasn't based on passion. It was based on commitment and the fact that he had given his word. I had him as my role model, and I knew that when I went to work in the marketplace, that was the ingredient I could bring to every single situation: when I say I will go to work for you, I will work for you.

It's amazing how many people go to work for someone else with the mistaken belief that the company exists to take care of them. I was raised with the belief that my job was to go to work and do what I was hired to do so my employer could make a lot of money, be profitable, and pay me. And as a kid who didn't have much growing up, that was my main motivation: to get paid.

One of my first jobs was trimming trees for a mobile home park in Muskogee that my grandfather lived in. He said, "Larry, I'll get you a job trimming trees for the guy who owns the trailer park. He will pay you $1.50 a tree." I was sixteen years old. I drove an old pickup, and I had a pair of hand trimmers and a saw. I went out and looked at the trees and thought, "These trees are only about six or eight feet tall; this shouldn't be too hard." There were about fifty trees so I knew that would be $75 which was enough to buy a couple of new pairs of jeans and go out on a date with my girlfriend. To me, this seemed like a great opportunity.

So, I took the job. When I got there, my grandfather said, "We're going to start at the back of the mobile home park, Larry," and he drove me around to the back. Those weren't eight-feet-tall trees around there; they were forty feet tall. It was $1.50 for cutting the limbs out of a forty-foot-tall tree that I had to climb to get to the top. I knew I was losing a lot of money on these tall trees, but a deal was a deal. The deal was $1.50 a tree regardless of how big the tree was, and I was raised to keep my word.

I did keep my word. I trimmed all fifty trees for $1.50 apiece. Some of them were eight feet tall, some were forty feet tall. But the valuable lesson that I learned, which I still hold more than fifty years later, is when you say you're going to do something, you do what you said you were going to do. You don't do it because it's convenient to do so or because it's such a good deal that you want to keep doing it. Sometimes you make a deal that sucks, but you do it simply because you said you would.

The fundamental point of my tree-trimming experience is that your values reflect how you do business. As I will emphasize throughout this book, your core values always show up in how you run a business. Show me your business and I will show you your values.

I've had lots of jobs in my lifetime. I drove a bookmobile in Muskogee and to many little surrounding towns. I set up book shelving in libraries around eastern Oklahoma. I did a lot of menial tasks to make a buck however I could, whenever I could. I started my work career by going door-to-door, selling strawberries that I picked from my folk's huge strawberry patch. I did anything I could to make money. And the thinking behind all of it was a really a very simple process: I wanted the money, and I was willing to do whatever it took to get that money, which meant that I was willing to do the work, regardless of what the work was. As long as it was legal, morally right, and I was physically able, then I was willing to do it so I could make the money so I could buy stuff. Stuff was always my big motivator. I wanted more stuff than I had. I didn't have much stuff and nobody I knew was willing or able to give me any stuff, so the only way to get more stuff was to work to earn the money to buy it.

And that process is how I learned to work for someone as well as figuring out what it took to be a successful entrepreneur. I became an entrepreneur the hard way; it was never really a part of the overall plan for my life. I started out with Southwestern Bell Telephone Company as one of the first male telephone operators in the state of Oklahoma. I did that because the hours were flexible. I could be a telephone operator all night, then get off work, drive to college, spend all day going to class, get out of class, have just enough time to catch a nap and do my homework, and go back to work that night as a telephone operator.

I worked my way up from being a telephone operator until twelve years later, when I became area sales manager in Wichita, Kansas. That was my transition within the Bell system—a pretty big leap from telephone operator to sales manager, and I was proud of what I was able to accomplish in my few years there. That was my career for the rest of my life as far as I was concerned until the Bell System broke up. It was called *divestiture*, and in effort to reduce the size of the workforce, they offered a buy-out based on your years of service.

I thought, "Wow, they're going to give me a year's pay to go away and do something else?" That sounded like a great deal to me! I didn't like living in Wichita much and I wanted to move back to Oklahoma so I took the deal. I didn't know what I was going to do, but I had a year's salary to tide me over which meant I had a little time to figure something out. I quickly got bored and had an opportunity to throw in with some guys to start a telecommunications company selling business telephone systems, as well as doing shared tenant services.

Shared tenant services meant you owned the telephone system within a big building and rented it out, as the telephone company used to do.

I started that business with these guys and was doing great: making lots of money, building the company up, hiring people, selling systems. It was a perfect scenario in every way, until one day the corporation commission ruled that what I did was no longer going to be allowed for new companies and my company didn't get grandfathered in. In other words, one day I went to work well-off, with a successful company, and left that day broke and bankrupt, with nothing. And while it didn't happen exactly overnight, but it sure didn't take long!

What was I going to do? I had no idea. I knew I could get another job selling telephones for someone else, but I also knew that wasn't going to make me happy in the long run. So, I thought long and hard about what I could do that would play off my strengths and would make me happy. One thing I had always been able to do was talk, and I'd always loved selling. So, I figured I could teach people how to sell. I didn't know anything about what it took to do that for a living, but I was determined to figure it out and be successful at it. I wrote several small sales courses on getting past the gatekeeper, handling objections, and closing the sale and other components of the sales process. I told myself that I would just sell these modules. Again, I didn't really know anything about professional speaking as a business model, but I knew how to sell, so I knew I could figure out how to make a living. I took the yellow pages in Tulsa; I began at the A's and started dialing for dollars.

These days, when people start their own business, they make the mistake of being unwilling to dial for dollars or take the product or service to the people. One of the biggest mistakes people make is buying into that stupid old cliché, "Build a better mousetrap, and the world will beat a path to your door." That belief has caused a lot of people to go broke, I can promise you.

Many entrepreneurs are such believers in their product that they actually believe that once they've got a website that tells people about it, they can sit back and wait for the money to roll in. It's not the case now, and certainly wasn't the case then. I knew if I was going to be successful, I had to take my product to the marketplace and not wait for them to come to me. So I started calling businesses and asked, "Do you have anybody doing any selling that I could talk to?" Even if they only had one person, I did my best to sell them my sales training program. I was selling these modules for $45. I figured that if I could sell six of those modules a day, six days a week, I could make a decent living and get by until I could raise my prices.

And that's what I did. I sold six modules a day, six days a week, to anybody who would listen to me. It didn't matter whether they had one salesperson or twenty-five. That's how I got started in professional speaking. (*Professional* just means you get paid.) I wasn't getting paid a lot, but I was still getting paid so I could call myself a professional speaker and was darn proud of it. That's how I became an entrepreneur—the hard way. I wasn't great at it when I started. I was worth just barely what I was getting paid. But I got better, and I kept at it. It was my passion that kept me going, it was my commitment to my family and my bills and myself.

Build It, and They Will Come? Nope

Today there's a lot of discussion about using visualization to bring success to you through the law of attraction and that type of woo-woo thinking.

People create dream boards with pictures of nice things: beautiful cars, great big houses, beautiful children, lots of money, boats, gorgeous locations to take vacations and the like. Do yourself a favor and make a reality dream board. The reality dream board should reflect what it's really going to look like. Imagine everything in the world going wrong, and then realize you haven't imagined nearly as bad as it's probably going to be. Am I saying that you should dream about it being horrible? No, I am saying that you should be realistic when it comes to picturing your future as an entrepreneur. You should know what it's going to look like. Picture the disappointment, the lack of money, the mistakes and failures. Know exactly what it will look like, so you won't be too surprised when those things actually happen. Too many people only picture the good things and believe that the bad things will never happen. That's naïve. The reality of starting a business is that it's worse than you're ever going to be able to imagine. It's tough out there in the real world and don't let anyone tell you otherwise.

I stand firmly against the law of attraction, with its "build it and they will come" attitude. Chances are things are not going to be OK. Chances are you're going to spend many nights lying in your bed thinking, "How the hell am I ever going to make it through another day? What do I tell my wife? What do I tell my husband? How do I explain this to my kids? How will this look to everyone I have bragged to? How do I explain this to my creditors?"

That's the reality of starting your own business. People sugarcoat it and say, "It's all going to be okay. Just get your vision board, and you'll make this happen." Or they say tell you to just go out there and create a great product." No, that's not enough either. I don't know any successful entrepreneur who has made it with just a good product or just a vision board or dream.

I am not much of an optimist, meaning that I hope things work out for the best, but I don't count or expect it. Instead, I am a realist, meaning that I do my homework and do the research and then do the math. And this kind of prep work always proves to be the right step. People let their emotions get in the way, especially when they want to follow their dream and follow their passion. But business is not an emotional venture, so, for the most part, people should keep their emotions out of it.

I look at the facts, and the facts are that very few people are going to make it in the long term by starting their own business. Overwhelmingly, most people should keep their day jobs and rely on someone else to make sure that the marketing and sales are done, the payroll is met, the taxes are paid, the doors stay open, and the lights stay on. Please, if you're not ready to do all of that, leave it to someone else who is more prepared. There is no shame in having a job and working for someone else.

Sadly, our culture these days has made *job* a dirty word. If you're not an entrepreneur trying to follow your passionate dream, others tend to say, "Oh, poor baby, how sad for you. You're still working for someone else." Having a job, working for someone else, and giving it your best, every single day is an honorable thing. People who are happy working for someone else aren't wrong for doing so. In fact, maybe they are the smart ones for understanding their skill set and their level of commitment and willingness. As a culture, we've got to stop shaming people for having a job and not wanting to be an entrepreneur.

However, for those who do want to be entrepreneurs and have done what it takes to stack the odds in their favor, I'm all for you! I will support you through the facts and skills it takes for you to fight your way through, to handle all the crappy things that will happen, and to make it in spite of them.

And what about love, passion and dreams? People say that you should follow your dream, find your passion and love what you do. Sounds so nice, doesn't it? After all, what could possibly be wrong with loving what you do? Since we spend so much of our lives working, shouldn't we love every minute of it?

If you figure out a way to do something you love, make a good living from doing it, and have financial freedom as the result of it then good for you. God bless you. But loving it is a bonus. Love cannot be the reason you go into business.

I know hearing that is probably going to upset many people because they believe that if they just find something they love then the money will follow. That idea has been really popular these last several years: find what you love, and the money will follow. That's just not true. You can love it all you want, but if you're not any good at it, nobody's going to pay you for it.

Dreams don't come true. We've told people to follow their dreams, but we didn't teach them how to create a plan and that's irresponsible. We must teach people how to create plans. My dream was to be successful and have financial freedom. I had to have a plan to get there so I could live my dream. And that came on the back of a written down plan and working hard on that plan to make it happen.

Years ago, I did a television show with Donny Deutsch called *The Big Idea*. He would bring entrepreneurs on the show and discuss what they were doing, their businesses, and their wonderful success stories. Every show had a theme. At the end of the show, he would bring someone on for what was called the "Millionaire Minute." It would be a discussion with a millionaire about the theme of the show.

Well, wouldn't you know it? I was asked to do the Millionaire Minute and the day I was on, the theme of the show was passion.

He said, "Larry, tell me how you feel about passion."

"Donny," I said, "passion is a total load of crap."

You could see the color drain away from Donny's face underneath all of that orange studio makeup as he shook his head and said, "Well, Larry, I don't agree with that."

"It doesn't matter whether you agree with it or not," I said. "I mean, it is your television show. You can be wrong if you want. But I know people who are passionate, and they are passionately incompetent." I went on to tell him that success was the result of hard work and excellence. Not just hard work and not just excellence but the combination of the two.

There are a lot of people in business who are passionate about what they do. They're just not any good at it. Passion doesn't equal quality. Passion doesn't equate to hard work, commitment, talent or skill. Passion is an emotion. YOUR emotion. Customers are not willing to pay for your emotion. One more time: success comes down to hard work and excellence. Too many people who followed their passion aren't willing to work hard, because they've bought into this silliness of "build it, and they will come" mentality. These people typically don't focus on excellence; they think that they can get by on their emotions instead of on the tangibles of a high-quality product, delivered in an excellent way, serviced well on the back end, and sold with appreciation and consideration for the customers and their wants and needs.

Those things are rarely addressed or even acknowledged when going into business, because society is selling people a bill of goods around following their passion.

The dictionary defines *passion* as "a barely controllable emotion." Don't believe me? Look it up for yourself. I for one don't want an emotion running my business. In fact, I don't want an emotion anywhere near my business. Any emotion. If you're going to pick one emotion, any emotion ought to make just as much sense. How about anger or rage? "I'm going to let rage run my business." Anybody I said that to would laugh and say, "Now you're being ridiculous." No more ridiculous than saying, "I'm passionate."

I want my business to make sense on paper because it has a tangible value in the eyes of the customer. Tangible, not emotional. I want my business to be based on quality, service, excellence, commitment, value and hard work. Emotions are fleeting and can't be counted on long-term. Emotions are the mood you are in at the time. Your mood. Show me a customer willing to pay for someone else's mood.

I watch The Food Network. I love watching people cook great food. I'm a pretty good cook myself and I'm always on the lookout for new recipes, ideas and techniques. I notice how a lot of chefs and cooks say, "What makes mine so good is that I cook with love! Love is my special ingredient. Take a bit of that and taste the love." No. Love is not an ingredient. Salt, pepper, garlic, sage, rosemary and thyme—those are ingredients. I can't taste love. You might love cooking but that is much different than cooking with love. Love is an emotion. It makes no tangible difference in the end result. The only way it matters is that you love what you do enough to become amazing at it.

A few years ago, I spoke to the National Barbecue Association. I love barbecue. I like to cook it and I like to eat it. I wandered around and talked to many famous barbecue pitmasters and listened to some of their presentations prior to my own keynote speech to group. In my speech, I told them that I had heard many of them talking about their passion for barbecue and how love was a special ingredient. I explained to them my position about love as an ingredient then told them that they were absolutely wrong about cooking with passion. I told them they couldn't afford to cook with passion, or they would end up going broke. I said, "I can cook with passion. You can't. Why? Because nobody is paying me for my barbecue. Whatever I cook, however I cook it, my friends and family will be fine with it. If you cook with passion and aren't amazing at everything that has to do with cooking your barbecue, your customers will not come back and will go on down the street to another barbecue joint." I don't believe many of them had thought about it in that way before.

By the way, did you ever notice that when people talk about their passion, they're only passionate if they're good at it?

I talk to professional speakers and coaches all the time. Part of how I make my living is working with people in this professional to help them move to the next level. They say, "I'm really passionate about helping people." Yeah, but your advice is really bad, and you suck at the business. Once they find that out that nobody is willing to pay them for their bad advice, which they suck at delivering, it's amazing how fast they lose the passion for helping people. People are only willing to stick with something and be passionate about it when they're pretty good at it.

I reserve my passion, my "barely controllable emotion," for my family. I love my wife and my kids and my grandkids. I love my dogs. I have a barely controllable emotion when it comes to all of those things. Beyond that, my business comes down to black-and-white. What are the numbers? If you're making money and having a pretty good time doing it, then you're doing all right. If you're not making any money, you ought to switch things up. Maybe you even ought to quit. Maybe you ought to keep your job. Because being profitable is what it's all about.

More people ought to be told to keep their emotions out of their business. Emotions will screw up how you hire, whom you hire and when you hire. Emotions will mess you up when things start to go to hell; they will stand in the way of your survival every single time.

Why? Because you will hang on longer than you should because of your emotions, and doing so just might cost you everything for the rest of your life.

The only emotions that matter are the customers' emotions. So yes, emotions do matter, but not yours. What is important is how the customer feels about what you do for a living. If the customer is passionate about what you do, woohoo! If the customer loves what you have to offer, that's wonderful. But too often, the entrepreneur loves it and is passionate about it and the customer is nothing but lukewarm. Result? You're done. You're out of business.

So be perfectly clear about this: The customer doesn't need your emotion. The customer doesn't need to know whether you love it or not. The customer doesn't need to hear how much passion you have for what you're doing. And you need to be absolutely clear that the customer doesn't care about how you feel; they need to understand the value you bring. Bring tangible value. Remember: Your passion about selling lawn mowers doesn't cut the grass.

Entrepreneurship as a Last Resort?

The title of the book clearly says not to quit your day job, but some people might be saying, "Larry, my day job quit me. I was laid off. I was furloughed. I have no idea whether my job will come back. I have no choice but to consider entrepreneurship or self-employment."

Is that a good enough reason to consider entrepreneurship—the feeling you don't have any other choices? "When your back is against the wall and you have no other choices, let's pick entrepreneurship." Does that make sense? Not to me it doesn't. Some folks mistakenly believe that when their back is against the wall, they will make the right decision. Chances are that's not true. We rarely make the best decision when we feel our only decision is to risk everything or when we've got nothing to lose. I can assure you that even when you've lost it all, there is more to lose. The safest, most conscientious, long-term thing you can do is always going to be to get a job.

Now I'm not saying to always play it safe or that it's always irresponsible to start your own business. I'm just saying to think first. If I were in a bind, I'd look to a job to save me, not something that has little chance of succeeding.

I deserve better. I'm sick of hearing people say, "I'm better than this." I'm sick of hearing about employers offering jobs to people who turn those tasks down because they believe they're too good to do what the job entails. Where does this sense of entitlement come from? You were hired to do the job, so do it. Never believe you are too good to work for a living and earn the money you are paid.

People need to be reminded of this: if you've got bills to pay, those bills are commitments. You said you would pay those bills; you didn't say you would pay them if everything was going really well. So you do what it takes to pay the bills, even when it's not your dream job, even when it doesn't fluff your aura, even if you hate it. If your job pays your bills and enables you to meet your commitments, you do it, simply because you said you would pay those bills. Your commitments drive your actions. Fulfilling your commitments, or doing what you said you would do, is an outward display of your inner core values. Your integrity is showing!

Two kinds of people

I believe there is always a job for someone who is willing to work. Nobody can convince me otherwise. We hear all these clichés growing up that life is divided between the haves and the have-nots. I don't believe that's true. I think that the world is instead divided between the wills and the will-nots. Will you do what it takes in order to keep your word? If your word is that important to you, you'll do whatever it takes. So . . . will you, or won't you? That's what it comes down to, not whether you have or have not, or whether you can or cannot. But always whether you will or will not. Chances are that you can, but the truth is that you won't.

Answer the question: Are you going to do what it takes no matter what? Or are you going to talk yourself into buying your own weak excuses? I rarely say, "Trust me" but you can trust me when I tell you that if you are looking for an excuse to not do something, you will always find one. You will tell yourself you are too old, too young, too poor, too busy and on and on and on. By the way, the dumbest excuse ever is the excuse that you are too busy. You aren't. Don't argue, you simply aren't. There is time. Plenty of time. More than enough time.

"But Larry, there are legitimate reasons that are not excuses." Yes, you are correct. I just don't want you to convince yourself that your excuses have magically transformed themselves into reasons. Reasons and excuses are very different, yet most folks are masters are turning their weak, flimsy, laughable excuses into solid, legitimate reasons. Don't be one of those people.

Use your time wisely

During the pandemic, a lot of people found themselves saying, "I've got some time on my hands. I'm home now. I have plenty of time to write out a business plan, think about what kind of business I would like to start, do some market research, improve my education, take some online courses, read books and ask questions of successful people. I've got plenty of time, and I choose to use this time to improve myself, so if I am able to start a business the right way. I want to capitalize on my downtime."

Not capitalizing on a slow time in your life when you have the opportunity to get more education and learn some new things would be a complete waste. We've always heard that old line, "Never waste a crisis." You would be wasting your crisis if you were not using that time to get smarter. If your dream is to own your own business, good for you. I encourage you, especially when you've got more time on your hands than you've had in the past to learn what you need to learn. Then when you start your own business, it's on your own terms and on solid ground and not because your back is against the wall and you're desperate. When you're desperate and you're thrashing around to survive, you're going to make lots of errors and blunders. Don't become an entrepreneur when you are in a desperate, emotional state. Instead, use every spare minute you can find to get prepared to become an entrepreneur the right way.

As I've already made clear, a very large percentage of businesses fail and fail quickly. You may look at those statistics and say, "But Larry, even if I have a passion about starting, with the odds not stacked in my favor why should I even begin?" Well, maybe you shouldn't.

People should definitely take the statistics seriously. They are based on history and represent what has happened to people who have started their own businesses.

So, before you take the plunge into being an entrepreneur, understand that only two-thirds of the people who start their own business are going to make it to the second year. In other words, a third of the people who start their own businesses today aren't going to be around 365 days from now. Are you still ready to risk it all? How about this: after five years, half of those who started their business today won't be here; in ten years, there's only going to be thirty percent of them left. I would pay close attention to those statistics and think carefully about what I need to know to make sure I am one of the few who can last.

So how did thirty percent of those folks who started their business figure out what it takes to survive in spite of themselves, in spite of the marketplace, in spite of a pandemic, in spite of stupid employees, bad hires, divorces, their kids' illnesses, deaths in the family, their own serious illnesses and all the other things that derail businesses? They were prepared. Probably not completely prepared—as you can never be completely prepared, but they weren't completely flying by the seat of their pants either.

Myths about Entrepreneurship

Let me conclude this chapter with some of the running myths about starting your own business. One of the things I hear most often when people talk about starting their own business is that they want to be their own boss. This is a completely ridiculous and laughable idea. You are never going to be your own boss, especially when you start your own business. Your name might be on the door and it may say CEO or President, but you aren't the boss and don't kid yourself into believing you are. It's always funny to me how solopreneurs print a business card that says, "CEO." It could just as easily say, "Janitor." They are the only employee, but they've got this delusion that they can be the CEO. They get into this mindset of "I get to be my own boss, and I'm going to be the best boss I have ever had." I promise you will be the worst boss you have ever had. Once you find out what being the boss really means, I will bet you that you don't really want to be your own boss. That old saying, "The buck stops here" is not an easy position to hold. I can assure you that you don't want to be the last person to blame. You always want someone else to blame. It's much better when you get to take all the crap that lands on your desk and put it on someone else's desk. If you are like most people and would rather do anything than take personal responsibility, then being the boss is going to really suck. Especially when you are taking responsibility for things you didn't even do. When you are the boss, it's all your fault, no one else's, just yours.

When you start your own company, it's just you. The boss is in charge of making sure there is money coming in constantly. The boss is in charge of every dime that comes in and every dime that goes out. The boss is in charge of making sure the employees get paid. And when payday is Friday and it's Thursday afternoon and the account is empty and you don't have the money to cover payroll, that's all on you. The boss is in charge of making sure that all the customers are happy and are being served well. The boss is in charge of making sure the taxes are paid, and the boss is the one who goes to jail if the taxes aren't paid. The boss has a lot of stuff going on that people never stop to consider. You had better make sure you are willing to do it before you say, "I want to be my own boss" because being a boss sucks in ways you haven't even begun to think about. That's what happens when you are blinded by the hype of entrepreneurism that is being sold by the podcasters and social media marketers. That's what happens when your passion gets out in front of your common sense.

Freedom!

The next big myth is that people want the freedom that comes from being an entrepreneur. Talk to any successful entrepreneur and ask them how free they are.

If they tell you they are, they are lying to you or they aren't really successful. You will have less freedom as an entrepreneur than you can ever imagine and certainly less freedom than you have when you have a job. If you want true freedom and income in exchange for a little bit of effort, get a government job where you go to work at nine o'clock on Monday, get your lunch break at twelve o'clock, get your two fifteen-minute breaks during the day and you go home at five o'clock. You do that again until Friday, when you get a nice paycheck. You will get insurance and other benefits like retirement and sick leave and vacation. And the best part of all of that is you will never have to worry about anything except doing the handful of things you were hired to do. You won't have to be responsible for anything except about half of what was in your job description. Now that's freedom.

There is no freedom in knowing that it's all up to you and you don't get to quit at five o'clock. You have to answer the phone and talk to your upset clients no matter when they call and no matter how petty their complaint is. You're always on-call. Go back to all of the things I said were part of being the boss, then double it and then figure out where your freedom is located on that list. There is no freedom that comes with entrepreneurship.

But if you're willing to give up your freedom, then being an entrepreneur might be just the right thing for you. Being an entrepreneur has many upsides, but don't think that freedom is going to be one of them because you are the one who is in charge of everything. That means you don't get to see your families often. You don't get to play with your kids. You're going to miss some games. You may miss some birthdays. Your spouse is going to miss you, and that will cause strain on the relationship and stress within the marriage. It's going to be a problem for all of your relationships. You're going to have to deal with the guilt, embarrassment, and shame of not being around the way you want to be, or even should be.

There is a huge price to be paid for being an entrepreneur when it comes to your time, energy, and especially your money, because your money is going to be rolled back into making your business work for a good long while. That's the sacrifice that comes from starting down the path of being a successful entrepreneur.

However, if you're willing to put up with all the crap you're going to have to put up with to make it, then the payoffs are huge. And if you make those sacrifices and figure out what it takes to make it and you fight the odds and win? Holy smokes, it is amazing! The biggest payoff for me is that I get to sit back, look at what I have been able to do and what I've been able to survive and say, "Look what I did!" There is nothing quite like the pride that comes from looking back at your accomplishments

2

Are You Really Ready?

After all I've done to discourage you from becoming an entrepreneur, are you still hanging in and want to move forward? If you are, then maybe you should re-read what I've said. Do you really believe that you are ready to become an entrepreneur or are you thinking you are more likely suited for the nine-to-five, day job lifestyle? Remember, the only wrong answer is to know you are suited for the job and risking it all by quitting your job and making the decision to become self-employed. If you are ready, then I'm going to help you get prepared because I want you to be one of the few who makes it.

If you're considering becoming an entrepreneur, do a little analysis of your life. Are you prone to take risks? If you are risk-averse and enjoy a feeling of safety, then being an entrepreneur is not for you. You should keep your day job and hang on to your nine-to-fiver. You should let someone else take the risks.

If you're scared to death every time the market goes up or down, you don't have any business being an entrepreneur.

Nor should you be an entrepreneur if you're afraid to talk to people. You should get a day job and sit in a cubicle somewhere. You've got to be open and outgoing and able to network. You have to be able to talk to people with confidence about what you do. The ability to speak well is a critical factor in entrepreneurial success. Are you afraid to speak in public? Keep your day job or get some coaching on how to speak effectively.

If you think selling is a hustle that takes advantage of people, you need to have a day job that's not in sales. Regardless of what your product or service is, selling is the key to success as an entrepreneur. It's always going to come down to selling every single time.

If you worry a lot, you probably shouldn't be an entrepreneur. If you tend to internalize problems and let them eat you up every time something goes wrong, you're going to be miserable as an entrepreneur, because most of the time, things will not be going well. That's a fact. Crisis and entrepreneurism are synonymous.

I know this sounds as if I'm trying to scare you off. Yes, I am. I don't want to see you invest all of your time, energy, and money and tell everyone, "I'm going to start my own business" when in twenty-four months your business is not going to be around. You're going to have to eat those words and they taste like crap! You're going to be broke, and chances are high that you will have spent your family's savings. That's a fact.

So yes, I am absolutely trying to scare you off. But when you get to the bottom of the funnel I'm creating, and you're one of the few left and can still say, "Wow. He didn't scare me off. I'm still ready," your chances of making it are going to be much higher than other people's chances. But if like most people who are at the top of the funnel you said, "Okay, I've had my business card printed, I've got my vision board and my dream and I'm passionate about what I do and I'm all ready to start my business," it is very likely you are not going to make it. Sorry. Save yourself some time and money and bail now. Send me a thank you later.

I'm asking you to do some self-assessment because you need to have the mental makeup to be able to last through the tough times. It's going to be a mental game as much as a financial game. You have to be ready to play the mental game of handling loss, frustration, and failure with not much to go on except hoping someday you'll have a win. Then you will build on that win until you find another win. And then you will have fifty more losses in a row. If you're not willing to do that, just keep your day job. At the beginning, there's a lot more losing than winning involved in becoming a successful entrepreneur.

A little more explanation: when I say, "Don't quit your day job," you could look at it two different ways. One meaning is, don't leave your job for the world of entrepreneurship or self-employment if you aren't suited for it and if you aren't ready to accept the reality. Stay in traditional employment. There's nothing wrong with working hard and adding value in a traditional job.

The other way to see it is, don't quit your day job until your new business is up and running and is on the road to sustainable success. Which means it is paying you enough to pay your bills and other financial commitments. This is also known as building your new business as a side hustle.

A side hustle can be a great way to start on the road to being a full-time entrepreneur. However, I have issues with some people's side hustles. If I am your employer and I am paying you to work nine-to-five, and your side hustle cuts into my nine-to-five, you're a thief because you're stealing time from me. Time that I am paying for that you are using to build your own business. I see this often in multilevel marketing (MLM) ventures. If you're working on your MLM business during the time I am paying you as your employer, that's an ethical issue. It means that you lack integrity. I am not paying your salary for you to work an hour or so a day on your side hustle. Your side hustle has to truly be on the side, outside of the time you're getting paid by someone else. So have integrity while you build your side hustle. That's the only way that I would ever support someone having a job and doing something else on the side. If they have the integrity to keep the two separate, the one who's paying your bills doesn't suffer while you build your new business.

From Paycheck to Profit

When you become an entrepreneur, you're going to have to make some major changes in the way you think. The first shift is moving from paycheck thinking to profit thinking. Who's showing up with the paycheck? As I said earlier, do you really want to be the boss? The boss is the one who makes sure the paycheck gets delivered on time.

Most entrepreneurs don't get a paycheck for a good long while. I went for a couple of years in my business before I ever took any money from the business because I was pouring every cent back into the business. For the first five years of my business, my employees made more money than I did.

I was fortunate in that I was married, and my wife was employed in a day job and could take care of the household expenses. Not everyone is that lucky. If you are the primary breadwinner, you don't have this luxury unless you are financially secure enough to pay your bills for a good long while. Can you afford not to have a regular paycheck coming in for a long time? If not, don't quit your day job. If you can afford it for a while, then you are going to have to get your mind focused on profitability. Figure out how to make money as quickly as possible so you can cashflow your business and not be funding it from your savings. Put all your energy into self-sufficiency. Keep your expenses low and spend your time on income-generating activities. You need to constantly ask yourself, "Is this action making me money?" If it's not, replace it with an action that is. And don't argue the point there are lots of activities that don't generate income that must be done. I know that. Do those expense-producing activities after you do the income-generating activities.

Calculate the amount of time you think it's going to take to start creating some income; then multiply that by three or four. It's going to take a lot longer than you think.

Profit is everything. These days I work with a lot of coaches, speakers, and entrepreneurs who brag about their six-figure business. Well, a six-figure business is a $100,000 business before taxes. In reality, that is not much money. You can make that much doing a lot of things that don't require the commitment or the risk. Is it worth it? When these people brag to me about their six-figure business, I often ask them how much they had to spend to make those six figures. It's amazing how many of them spend more than $100,000 to make their $100,000. That's not a business; that's an expensive hobby.

Then there's the matter of making a shift from a time-and-effort mentality to a 100 percent earned-results mentality.

Results are everything. It's not what you're working on, it's what you are getting done. It's not how many people are the in pipeline, it's how many sales you have made. We all get caught up in the busyness of running our business. We don't focus nearly enough on whether it's making us any money. Results make you money; everything else is just keeping you busy. Understanding that simple statement will make you look at what you're doing much differently.

I do a lot of coaching with small businesses. I ask them, "What are you doing right now?"

"Well, I'm working on my website. I'm really working hard." No, you're staying really busy; there's a difference. You're not making any money. You're not talking to customers. You aren't doing any income-generating work.

However, these folks have convinced themselves that their website eventually can drive traffic to their business and that it needs their immediate attention. Yes, the website needs attention, but not immediate attention.

It's passive marketing. It's not selling. Selling generates income.

If you're in trouble—and for the first several years you're going to be in trouble—you need to be doing only activities that bring in income. Begin to assess every single thing that you're doing and ask, "Is it making me money, or is it just keeping me busy?"

Busyness, the kind of work that's not bringing in money, is the costliest item on your expense sheet. Here's a rule for me: If something can slide, let it slide. The only things that can't slide are income-earning opportunities and activities. Those things never get to slide. Never, never, never. I've been doing my business for thirty years. If I have an opportunity to do something that earns money, I drop everything and focus on that opportunity. I will push to the back burner anything that doesn't earn me money, because still, after thirty years, I understand that it's the income-earning opportunity that keeps me paid on Fridays, keeps my employee paid, and keeps the doors open and the lights on. Memorize this: If it doesn't make me money, let it slide. If it makes me money, do it now.

You're going to have to shift your thinking from merely being about time and effort. Time and effort are how you measure things when somebody else is paying you. You're getting paid just to show up, and you're not really going to be asked, "You were here this many hours.

Let's talk about how much revenue you brought into the business to make sure you're paying for yourself and contributing enough to make your employment make sense to me."

That's not going to happen if you've got a job. It happens every single day, typically several times a day, if you're running your own show. That's why people have to expand their thinking from time and effort to time, effort and profitability. You're running your own show. Everything you do, from the time you decide that you're on the clock to the time you quit, everything has to be looked at in terms of "Is it making me income, revenue, profit?"

Subscription entrepreneurism

Seems like there is more of this going on than ever, especially in the Internet marketing world, where people are selling programs online. They build an online program for thousands and thousands of dollars. They shoot videos, record audios, produces pdfs, create the marketing materials. They convince themselves this is just the ticket to getting rich. They say to themselves, "It's only $17 a month. I will get a thousand people to pay me $17 a month and I will make $17,000 a month. All I would have is the cost of my website, and I'd have to do some online delivery of coaching via audio, video and Zoom." Simple plan. Should work. And thousands and thousands of folks are trying to make this model profitable. Some do. Most don't. I say to those who bring these ideas to me, "You're absolutely right. If you get a thousand people and make $17,000 a month, that's great. How are you going to sell three? Just tell me how you are going to sell the first three?

"What do you mean?" Just explain to me in detail right now how you're going to sell the first three. Then we can talk about how you're going to sell a thousand.

It's hard to sell a thousand people anything. No matter how good it looks on paper, or what you have convinced yourself you can pull off, making it happen is almost impossible.

Think like an Employee

Some authors suggest that the biggest challenge for becoming an entrepreneur is to get people who have been employees their entire working life to start thinking like an owner.

Actually, I'm not big on thinking like an owner. I believe that you have to think like an employee forever. You are an employee of your bottom line. Your bottom line is my boss. Every day, the bottom line determines your activities, just as a boss determines the activities of their employees. A good boss determines what should be done, what you can let slide, what you have to do to take care of customers, and what you have to do to make sure that the company remains profitable. The boss determines when it has to be done and how it should be done.

When you are running your own business, you're the boss in the sense that your name is on the door and you have the business card that backs it up. But what really runs your company should be your bottom line. If you're not profitable, your activities have to change in order to drive profits. What you do, when you do it, and how you do it is determined by your bottom line—your profitability.

This is exactly how it works for me in my own business. Every single day my profitability determines my activities. My boss is the bottom line. If I don't have the money to pay the bills or make payroll, I've got to shift my activities to make sure I can. The reason I run a successful business is because I know who I work for. I am the employee of the bottom line. If you want to be a successful entrepreneur, then you are going to have to stop thinking like the owner and start being the employee of the bottom line.

Okay, now that you are clear who you work for, you have to know who is in charge of your bottom line. The bottom line is primarily determined by the customer. There's an old line from Sam Walton, founder of

Walmart: "The customer is the ultimate boss and can fire everybody from the CEO to the janitor."

The customer's money provides you with the revenue. If the revenue is not there, you've got to ask what you can do in terms of your efforts, your activities, your service to others and the value you provide to make sure the revenue is there. The revenue is always the driver, and it's in the hands of the customer.

Never Spend All Your Money

According to a US Bank study, 82% of businesses fail due to poor cash flow management. Does that tell you just how important it is to pay close attention to your money? Most don't. Most entrepreneurs spend every cent that comes through the door. One of the rules of being a successful entrepreneur, is to understand that you should expect the unexpected. Always. You've got to have some money set aside to handle yourself through that.

In terms of personal finances, if people would only have six months of their expenses set aside in savings, they would be able to handle just about every financial crisis of the last hundred years. They would have been able to last through the 2008 real estate downturn, because most people only got in trouble about three months into the crisis. In the pandemic of 2020, if people would have had six months of their expenses set aside, they wouldn't have missed their paychecks on Friday and been standing in food lines on Tuesday.

People rarely have enough money set aside. If you're an entrepreneur or solopreneur, you have to be constantly setting money aside so when something happens you have the financial reserves to weather the storm. And please don't be so naïve to think something won't happen. Something always happens. Always. You are not immune to disaster. So expect the best but prepare for the worst.

When you are first starting your new business don't overpay for things that you can do yourself. Many entrepreneurs hire too fast and spend too much to make sure that their logo is perfect, and their website is pretty. They hire a photographer, a branding expert, an accountability coach and the list goes on and on. A lot of times they are turning to other people for things that they could put off for a while or they could learn to do themselves. I am not against any of these things, I am just saying that you need to turn to yourself and do everything you can do before you hire other people to do it for you. You are your own first best answer.

Before you spend too much too fast, do your homework. Is this revenue-producing? If it's revenue-producing, do it. Don't convince yourself that picking the right color for your brand or logo or website is revenue-producing, because it's not. Brand is just what people say about you when you're not around. Don't convince yourself that a new photo from a photographer is revenue-producing, because chances are it's not. Go back to what I've said several times already and ask yourself if what you are doing is making you money. Make sure you know that what makes you money is asking customers to buy from you and do business with you. Get in front of people, because it's people who have the money that drives the business that enables you to do all of these other things.

Have the Law on Your Side

Starting a new business requires legal counsel. When people are employees, probably the worst thing they have to worry about is losing their jobs. Employees usually don't have to worry about getting sued. They're protected as employees who are part of an organization. But when you are the owner, you have to consider how your decisions might affect your company legally. We live in a litigious society. People love to sue. If someone can sue you for any kind of real or even imagined hurt, they probably will. You are going to need a good lawyer to set up your business. You need a good tax person so you're setting your business up the way to be most advantageous to you down the road in terms of taxes.

Don't start out thinking you can do this on your own. You don't want to get sued and lose all of your personal assets while you're putting together your business. So find a good attorney and a good tax person. Both of these people are absolutely critical to your success.

Pay your taxes. Don't say, "I'll put my taxes off, because I've got this bill or that bill to pay," or "I need to buy a piece of equipment." I'm telling you, pay your taxes first. The government will get its money. Notice I said *its* money. It's not your money, it's their money. They are going to get their money no matter what.

By the way, whether you like it or not, the government deserves its money. The government enables you to be in business in the first place. Jim Rohn, world-renowned speaker and author always said that the government is the goose that laid the golden egg and you've got to feed the goose. Yes, the goose eats too much. Yes, the goose can become a pig sometimes. Yes, the goose can make a mess wherever it goes. But our wonderful, capitalistic, entrepreneurial society is our goose. Our taxes pay to feed that golden goose. I'm very appreciative of the fact that I live in a country where I can start and build a business and reap the benefits of that business. Never cheat the goose that laid the golden egg or try to starve it. Feel honored that you have the ability to start your own business and earn money. Don't be resentful of a society that allows you to do that.

Entrepreneurship and Family

Entrepreneurial life can be a hard on your family for sure. And in the beginning, it can be a real shock to families who may be used to you having a more predictable nine-to-five schedule.

I don't believe it's ever truly possible to prepare your loved ones for what's ahead when you start your own business. After all, you don't fully know what's ahead either. However, you can warn your family of what they can probably expect.

Many things come at you when you're starting your own business. And since the buck stops with you, it's up to you to make sure those things are taken care of. These things are going to take up a lot of your time, energy, effort, and emotions. And you only have so much of those things to offer.

That means something's got to give. When you give all your emotions and energy and time to fixing your business, something will suffer. It's going to be your family. You're going to have to have a frank, open, and honest discussion with your partner and maybe with your kids depending upon how old they are. If you don't have a rock-solid relationship with your partner, starting and succeeding in a new business is going to be much harder for you. While being an entrepreneur is lonely, you aren't in it alone. Don't be selfish and think this is just your business you are starting. Everyone in your family will pay a price for you starting your own business. They are your partners, not just your family, so involve them.

A good business is built on the foundation of the person who starts it, and a major part of every person's foundation is their relationships.

If you are taking care of your parents, your decision is going to affect your parents. Many people in the sandwich generation have kids of their own while they are taking care of their parents. Going into business will affect all of those relationships, and it's certainly going to affect your relationship with your spouse or partner.

You're going to have to prepare your family for the worst. It's great to bring them in on your dream of how wonderful it's going to be, but you've got to prepare them for the fact that it's probably going to suck for a while. It's going to suck when you can least afford it to suck. You're going to have lots of conversations with those closest to you during these times. You need to vent and so do they. When you're in one of those situations where you're trying to bail the water just to keep the boat afloat, you'll have to remind them that this is what you warned them about.

You can't expect your loved ones to have your back every single time. This is scary stuff with a lot at stake. So don't let what's coming be a surprise. It's not fair to your spouse to say, "This is all going to be great," and then not have it turn out great. You've got to prepare them with a realistic conversation of what becoming an entrepreneur really means to every aspect of your married life, family life, parenting and finances.

Have the hard conversations. Have those conversations about your time. Have those conversations about money. As I've already told you, there are going to be times when the money is just not there. The money has to go back into the business. Make a commitment to make it as easy as you can for those around you. Remember, even though it may look like a nightmare from time to time, you are following your dream, but it's probably not their dream.

There will be lots of hard conversations, and it's fair to have a spouse or a partner or your kids come to you saying, "Why don't you just go back to your day job?" That may be an option for you. Maybe it's even a good idea. Later on, I'm going to talk about when it's time to let it go.

It would be a shame to run a successful business and lose your family in the process. That's not success. It would be a shame to say, "Look at what I've built. I've got my company up and running smoothly and I'm making lots of money" but you sacrificed your health in the process. It would be a shame to sacrifice your sanity. You've got to take care of your sanity and the sanity of those around you. Your business can make you frustrated, that is to be expected. But your business can't make you crazy. You can't allow that. And that's what happens to many. They become so obsessed with their business that they lose what's really important. Your health, your sanity and your family are the most important things in your life. Not your business. Your business is there to provide the financial means for you to live the life you want to live. It's not there to take your life and loved ones from you or to take you from them. Too many people sacrifice themselves physically as well as mentally in order to follow their dream and build a business.

Celebrate It All

I've already made it pretty clear that even with the best of planning and the best of intentions, unexpected things are going to occur. So your question might be, how do you prepare for what you can't prepare for? I'm not sure you can, except to know that it will happen. For me, I've always found some level of satisfaction in knowing that things are going to happen, even when what is going to happen isn't a good thing. The awareness alone can steel your nerves and make you stronger.

When I first started in the professional speaking industry, I was a sales trainer. As time went on and I spent more time on stages, I developed into more of a motivational guy.

One of the first products I produced to sell at the back of the room after my speeches was a bumper sticker that said, "Expect the best. Be prepared for the worst. Celebrate it all." I've always approached everything I do with that as one of my mantras.

Expect the best: I really do expect that my efforts will pay off. The reason I am able to expect the best is because I know I am prepared when I begin something. I know that I am committed to doing my best and working hard and that I am resilient when things don't go well. But in expecting the best, I have also always been prepared for the worst. I prepare financially, mentally, emotionally and psychologically. I know that even with the best of preparations that everything to go to hell at any moment and that knowledge alone is part of being prepared.

I know some people will respond to this with, "Larry, that's a very pessimistic way to look at things. If you're always expecting for things to go to hell at any moment, aren't you setting yourself up for failure?" Not at all. In fact, just the opposite is true. And I understand that old law of physics: what goes up must come down. When things are going really great, that's typically when they fall apart for you.

I've always been prepared for things to fall apart, and it has never worried me much, because I've had the skills and a plan for what to do when it happens. I know how to circle the wagons, regroup, and start again. I know how to scrap it, start over, and figure out something new. I know how to take it to the streets to make revenue come in instantly. I know how to do those things because I learned how to do those things, and I also know what happens when you don't know how to do those things. I have always expected the best, but I have always been prepared for the worst. Then I learned the line that brings sanity to the process: celebrate it all. Just make an agreement with yourself that you are going to enjoy the ride as best you can. Know that getting pissed off and miserable doesn't fix anything. In fact, it only makes it worse. So slap a big old fake smile on your face, be glad you are still alive and can fight another day and get your butt back to work. Chances are good that you can figure out what you need to do but whining about it isn't going to get you there. Blame won't get you there. However, awareness, acceptance, determination, commitment, and hard work will get you there.

Make sure to spend time gathering the skills so you can do what I've just talked about. I am constantly educating myself. When I was first in this business, I said, "If I'm going to be a professional speaker, I need to know everything every professional speaker who's making a dime out there is saying and how they are saying it."

Thirty years ago, the best way to do that was to buy audiotapes from Nightingale-Conant, because they were the king of audio learning. I listened to over five thousand hours of audiotapes from the world's leading speakers. That's how I could know what they were saying, how they were saying it, and how they could mix humor and entertainment with content and information. I listened to the differences in styles. I called as many of them as I could find access to. Some would talk to me, some wouldn't. I bought every book I could find on personal development, business, selling, customer service and leadership. Before I ever wrote a book on any topic, I read the top 100 bestselling books on that topic because I wanted to have research on that topic. In the past thirty-five years, I've read thousands of books and I can assure you those books and the education I received from them have been the biggest differentiator between me and most of the marketplace. Over the years, I gained a depth of research and personal experience that enabled me to say the things I say right now. That constant education has given me the skills to pivot and turn when things go wrong.

While you can't be prepared for everything that might happen, you can acquire the skills and resources that will keep you from being devastated by what might happen.

There was no way that the businesses in the United States or around the world were ever going to be prepared for a global coronavirus pandemic. It had never happened before, and it caught the world by surprise.

While business owners were not prepared for the pandemic, they could have been prepared for "something bad to happen" by having six months' worth of expenses set aside. They couldn't have been prepared for the coronavirus, but they could have been prepared for something—coronavirus, economic downturn, horrible weather. It doesn't matter what you call it or what caused it. Bad happens. Be prepared. I learned that motto as a small boy when I was a Boy Scout: be prepared. For what? It doesn't matter. Just be prepared. Be prepared for any horrible thing that might happen to you by having an expectation that it might. Preparedness begins when you stop being naïve.

I don't know what's going to happen, but I know that something's going to happen. I know that when it happens, I have skills to fall back on. I have some education. I have worked on my skills. I know what I can do. I have a plan B. Can you say the same thing? If not, I would fix that as quickly as possible.

You also have to surround yourself with a network of trusted people. People you can trust with your problems and who are trustworthy enough to keep it to themselves. And people you can trust to kick your butt when you've been stupid, hold your hand when you're hurting and celebrate with you when things are great.

I have a handful of people like this. We've been buddies for thirty years. When COVID-19 hit in March of 2020 and we were all locked down in our houses, my buddies agreed that every Friday afternoon we were going to have a happy hour together online. And we have never missed a Friday since that day. We show up with a cocktail and talk about our lives and our businesses and our feelings. We laugh and tell old stories that we've heard many times from each other. What we talk about isn't that important. What's important is that we are there for each other and we all know it.

This is a very special thing that isn't often found. Rarely do people work to nurture friendships to build trust like we have. And notice that I used the word *work*. Relationships are work. They require time and commitment. And they can save your life when you are in trouble by giving you people you can go to for help, advice, or even just an ear to listen to you.

Everybody should be working to build a network so that when things go bad, you don't feel so alone. Being an entrepreneur, especially a solopreneur, is lonely. You don't have a board of directors. You don't have a bunch of vice-presidents you can call in and say, "Let's talk about this and come up with a plan of action." For the most part, it's just you and the mirror. If you can establish even a tiny network of trusted individuals you can talk to, you and your business will benefit in ways you can't imagine.

In addition to building a network of trusted friends, you can hire a coach. Now, I have to admit I hesitate to write these words. Why? Because it seems like every-body and their dog is a coach these days. Calling your-self a coach doesn't make you a coach. I can call myself a giraffe, but it doesn't mean I've got a long neck!

Be careful when you hire a coach. Coaches should be experts in the area or areas where you are not an expert. I teach coaches how to speak better and help them to better voice their expertise and I have become very involved in the coaching industry in the past several years. I teach coaches that you must use your depth of experience as well as your depth of research. And I make it clear that your own experience is not research. Just because you did it and went through it a certain way, doesn't mean that way can be validated by research. It just means you did it that way. Too many coaches are teaching how they did it and think that's the way it's done. This applies to any and all topics. This is how I branded my business, so this is how you should brand your business. This is how I lost weight so this is how you should lose weight. That's a coach but it's not a great coach. A great coach uses their experience as well as their research.

When I coach a small business, it's because I have run several small businesses and have experience. I've also interviewed and worked with hundreds and hun-dreds of businesses over the years. I have studied busi-ness success and what to do when you are struggling in different areas of your business. In other words, I have done my research. I can listen to what you are dealing with, ask good questions, give you a solid plan with specific strategies and tactics to get you out of the mess you are in and I can hold you accountable to make sure you get it done. I'm a good coach.

You want a good coach. A good coach can save you lots of time because they've been there, done that, and know what to do next. So, if you are thinking of hiring a coach, make sure that's the case. Find out if the coach has experience and has done their research. Make sure the coach you work with knows what they are talking about. Make sure they can back up their words with results in their own and life and business as well as in the lives and businesses of the people they have worked with. Never hire a broke person to teach you how to get rich. That's just common sense.

Remember that the language of the Internet is hyperbole. Hyperbole means exaggerated claims. It's easy for someone to say whatever they want to say about themselves on the Internet or social media. And they do. They make claims of all they have done and how they've done it. How do you know what's true? There is no truth enforcer on the Internet. Nor should there be. Buyer beware! Do your own research. Just because a product claims to be the best, doesn't make that product the best. Coaches are a product. They can claim to be the best without having the best results. It's up to you to make sure they are telling the truth.

Coaches can be a great help. A good one is worth more than you can imagine. A bad one is a waste of time and money.

Don't get caught up in the hyperbole of their marketing. Don't hire someone to do what you can do for yourself. Don't hesitate to ask tough questions about the coach you are considering.

3

Why Does A Business Exist?

Ask most people, "What are you owed by the business you work for?" and they will probably say, "They owe me a fair wage."

Okay, that seems fair. A fair wage is a popular topic today and we hear a lot about what constitutes a fair wage. Business leaders, labor unions and politicians all have their opinion of what's fair. I believe that any wage that you agreed upon when you were hired is fair. You entered into the agreement when you took the job and thought it was fair. After all, why would anyone willingly enter into an agreement that they didn't think was fair? That doesn't even make sense! Don't take a job for a wage and then complain that that the money you agreed to be enough now isn't, just because you've adjusted your lifestyle to the point where you need more money to pay your bills. You made a deal, and a deal is a deal. This assumes of course that over time your wage has been adjusted based on the cost of living going up across the country. Just because you adjusted your style of living and bought a new car, or moved to a bigger house, or spend more money than you earn, that doesn't mean it's your employer's responsibility to keep paying you more so you can keep up.

There's a sense of entitlement prevalent in the minds of many that the company exists to pay people enough to live any way they choose to. That sense of entitlement is destroying our society and killing businesses. It seems that some expect employers to assume the role of mama and daddy when it comes to taking care of their employees. When people believe it is the role of businesses to take care of employees regardless of the employee's personal choices it allows employees to abdicate personal responsibility for living on what they agreed to be paid. Just because the employee's financial situation changed doesn't mean that the company bears any responsibility for that change.

Secondly, many people believe that the business is there to take care of them not only financially but emotionally. Too many employees never want to get their feelings hurt. They believe the company should shelter them in every way from the stupidity of those they work with. Don't believe me? Turn on the news or go to the

Internet and read what people are upset about. And I am not talking about sexual harassment or racial slurs or any of the other things that are clearly wrong or illegal. Those things should never take place.

Think back to your family. Could your mama and daddy guarantee you that your brat brother wasn't going to say something stupid to you and make you cry? No, because your brat brother was just a jerk and said stupid things to everybody. He's probably still saying stupid things to people and hurting their feelings.

Some people just say stupid things. A business is not there to protect you from the stupid things other people say. They can write policies and have meetings all day long and some bozo will still say something dumb. Your employer cannot be responsible for your emotions or your feelings. That goes back to personal responsibility. You are responsible for your feelings. Your employer is responsible for keeping you physically safe, but your emotions are always going to be up to you.

We've reached a sad place in society where too many believe their employer exists to serve them instead of the other way around. The role of the employer is to compensate you for the amount of effort and time you provide based on what was originally agreed upon when you took the job. If you are providing more than what was agreed to originally, then have a new discussion and come to a new agreement where they agree to compensate you more. But be clear that they don't owe you a safe space where you are never going to get your feelings hurt or always going to have enough money to pay your bills.

The One Big Reason!

Businesses exist for one reason only and that is to be profitable. That's the only reason a business ever goes into business. Most businesses fail because they lose sight of that reason. As I've said several times already, the activities that generate revenue are the most important activities for any entrepreneur to focus on. The bottom line is the real boss. When you abandon that boss, when you fail to honor the revenue and the customer who brings the revenue in, you are bound to fail.

Businesses exist to be profitable. Those profits pay employees. Employees would be well-served to remember that the business that pays them has to be profitable in order for their paychecks to clear.

As an entrepreneur, you have to keep it foremost in your mind that your business exists to be profitable. You can never forget, even for a moment, that the reason you started your company, invested your time, energy and money as well as your blood, sweat and tears, was to be profitable. Period. Profitability rules. I never understand when I hear someone say they are starting a business and money isn't all that important. Okay, I admire people who are independently wealthy and want to serve others and bring value to the marketplace and have no need for the enterprise to be profitable. I think that's great. But let's not call that a business. And let's not confuse that with the situation of most who start a business. Most people become entrepreneurs with the idea of making money.

Surprisingly, there are many people today have an issue with making lots of money. I have never figured this one out. Somehow, they think making money is rooted in greed and deceit and people who have it must be taking advantage of others in order to makes lots of it. If you identified with that statement in any way, rethink your plans to become an entrepreneur. If you have guilt around earning money, you have no business being an entrepreneur.

I've never felt guilty about earning money because I know I provided value, and the customer has shared their money with me based on the value I brought to them. It was an exchange of value. They valued the solution I brought to their problem more than they valued the money they had to pay to get my solution. That's what business is: an exchange of value.

The money you receive for solving a problem the customer has is honorable money. You earned it. You worked for it. There is nothing to feel badly about. You made money by bringing value and solving a problem. That's exactly the way it's all supposed to work!

If you did all of that and got paid good money for it and it cost you less to provide it than you made, that is profit! Woohoo! Profit is the reason you went into business to begin with, right? Profitability keeps you afloat. It pays others. It pays to feed the golden goose. It takes care of your family. It allows you to buy stuff which takes care of the families who produced that stuff and the ones who sold you that stuff. It's a wonderful thing. That's why it deserves your utmost respect and all of your attention and should be honored in every way. If you don't, then profitability goes away. And once you lose profitability, you've got to shut it down and go back to your nine-to-five. It's that simple.

Changing the world

It's amazing to me how people say, "I really want to change the world." Guess what? The world doesn't want to change. Think of all the businesses that started out to change the world, and yet look at the shape the world is in.

The world changes when it wants to change, not because you started a business. The world is the way it is. Except . . . solving a customer's problem changes their world. Even if all you did was sell them a candy bar, for a few moments while they were enjoying that candy bar, their world changed in a small, sweet, delicious way. And you made money doing it. They had a delicious experience, and you made some money. You will pass that money on to others. In that way, the world changes just a tiny bit with every profitable transaction of service you provide and the little bit of value you bring to the marketplace.

I come from the world of personal development and self-help. Many speakers in this niche are convinced they have the ability to change people's lives. That's not true. People change their lives when they want to change, not when you want them to change. To say that you are changing lives is rooted in arrogance. All that anyone can do is change their own life and hope you can be an example to a few others and that in turn, they will make some small changes in their own life and on and on it goes.

I got into the self-help business to help myself. I provide value to people and they compensate me for that value. As you read this right now, hopefully you're going to get value from the words that I'm sharing here. But notice that you had to pay to access these words. I don't feel badly because you had to pay to read words that will help you live a better life, run a better business, make more money, be more profitable, and serve other people better. I earned that money you paid. I provided value and solved a problem and you paid for the solution.

Do I end up winning in the end? Absolutely. But don't you also win? You got advice that can help you and I sold the advice that can help me. You will get more benefit than the few dollars you paid for the advice. Big value for you. I will get more money than it cost me to provide the advice. Big value for me. A double win. And does the world change? In this way, you will run a better business and employ people. You will buy stuff. Same for me. That's capitalism at work.

I didn't start my business to lose money; I started it to earn money. People can lose focus about the reasons they are starting their business. Yes, you can be charitable. In fact, you should be. I believe charity is required from all of us. To whom much is given, much is required. That statement, while biblical, is well beyond biblical; it's simply the right thing to do. You are a better human being when you share part of what you have with other people. The more you have, the more you have to share. The more money you earn, the more you can give away. Something ultimately very good comes from earning a lot of money. The focus of your efforts should be to be profitable, because profit runs everything, including charity and that is how being a successful business owner changes the world.

The Great Idea fallacy

How many times have you heard someone say: "Boy, I have a great idea!" They are so excited and pumped up about what they believe is a revolutionary idea. *Shark Tank* is one of my favorite television shows. You've probably seen it. Aspiring entrepreneurs step in front of the sharks with their idea in an attempt to create enthusiasm for the panel of multi-millionaires and billionaires to invest in. Sometimes their enthusiasm in almost nauseating to me because it's so over the top. I appreciate enthusiasm but enthusiasm alone doesn't make any of the sharks pull out their checkbook. It's the business plan, the units sold, the cost of goods, the debt, the person and their experience and research, the competitive arena they are entering, and ultimately their profitability. Is this stuff hitting home with you yet? Broken record, right? I keep coming back to this because it's the stuff most people overlook. Enthusiasm isn't enough. Passion won't get you there. Even a great idea won't get you across the finish line and guarantee your success. None of those things are enough to determine whether your business is really going to be necessary and survive and thrive in the marketplace.

There are many great ideas and most of them should never be turned into products or into a business because there's no money in them. A great idea does not guarantee you success. Lots of great ideas have failed. And lots of stupid ideas have made a ton of money. You might be thinking "that's not fair! Good ideas don't do well, and stupid ideas can do great?" Yep. That's a fact. By the way, who promised you fair?

Remember the Pet Rock fad back in the seventies? Probably not, but I'm old and I do remember it. The Pet Rock can tell you what the weather is going to be like. Yep, the Pet Rock told you what the weather was. You set your rock outside, and if it gets wet, it's raining. If your rock gets hot, the sun is shining. If your rock gets cold, it's cold outside. Stupid, huh? That stupid idea that made a ton of money. Never believe that the quality of the idea alone is directly proportionate to the quality of its marketability, or that it will determine how much money the idea is going to make.

Never underestimate the power and profitability of making something fun or cool. But if I really wanted to assure my long-term success as a business owner, I would focus on solving a tangible problem over the fun or cool factor. But don't kid yourself about how much the world needs what you've got. I am betting that the world is just fine without what you are offering. And I'm also betting that the world can probably find what you are offering from someone else at a lower price. Ouch! That sucks to hear, doesn't it? It's still true. So what are you going to do?

When we look at our product or service, most of us tend to believe that we are so unique that people can't live without what we offer. We don't tell ourselves the truth that most likely, everyone is going to be just fine without it. If you understand that nobody really needs what you've got and will live happy fulfilled lives without having ever heard of you or your business, then you have a better understanding of reality. You will market it in such a way that it satisfies a customer's desires based on what they perceive to be a problem that creates pain in their life or business. You will understand that this pain costs them something, and the cost of dealing with the pain is higher than the cost of your solution. (That is the fundamental principle of sales, by the way.) Entrepreneurs who say, "The world's got to have this" are only fooling themselves. The absolute truth is that the world is going to be just fine without it.

On being Larry Winget

From the beginning of the motivational speaking industry, there was a way that business was done. The folks who did it were all pretty much the same. It was hard to tell one from the other. They wore the same kind of suit. They told the same kind of jokes. They had basically the same lineup of topics: attitude, goal setting, creating a vision, discipline, commitment, hard work and on and on.

I started out as that kind of motivational speaker. You really couldn't tell me from anyone else. I looked like the rest of them and I sounded much like the rest of them.

That was because I had studied them for so long. I listened to audios of their speeches. I watched their videos. I knew what other speakers were doing. I knew what worked in the motivational speaking industry. I knew the kind of suit I was expected to wear and the kind of jokes I was expected to tell. "Do what the masters do, and your chances of becoming a master go way up." That's a universal law.

I did what the masters had done, and as my chances of becoming a master increased I became pretty successful as a motivational speaker. But—and it was a big but—I felt an internal lack of authenticity. Every day I would put on my motivational speaker suit and do my motivational speech talking about all the same principles that every other motivational speaker was talking about. I was just a slightly different version of it. Same car, same engine, just a different color and a different model.

By the way, I'm not just talking about my speaking career here; I'm talking about any business and every business. When we all look alike and sound alike, and all of our products and services are pretty much alike, the client or customer can't really tell us apart. When the client can't tell us apart, we end up competing on the basis of price. That is a losing proposition. Anyone can be a nickel cheaper making them the best choice.

I didn't want to compete on price, and I didn't want to look or sound like everyone else. I didn't want to be a commodity. Besides, even though I was experiencing real success financially, I realized that what I was saying just didn't feel right. I didn't believe most of the motivational clichés that were being said on stages all over the world. Even though the multitudes were buying them, I knew in my gut they weren't true—at least they weren't true for me.

I don't believe that a positive attitude is the key to everything. Motivational speakers say that attitude is everything, and books are written saying that, and you can go to your favorite podcast channel right now and find that that topic gets a lot of interest. But it's not true. I am a big proponent of negativity. There is definitely a time when you have to get negative. There is a time when you need to get negative about your life, your situation, your business, your finances, and your relationships. A time when you need to get negative about weight and your health. When you get negative and I mean negative to the point that you make yourself sick about where you are, that's when you will become willing do whatever it takes to create positive change. But in the world of personal development, no one was telling anybody to get negative. Everybody was saying, "Be positive." Not my style at all—so I went a different direction.

And that's just one example of the conflict I was going through with my message, and ultimately my business being out of alignment with my beliefs and values. The motivational clichés and platitudes weren't working for me. I had to make a big decision. I had to decide whether I was going to shift my entire business, my brand, my look, my message and go in the totally opposite direction. Was I really willing to walk away from what had proven to be successful and profitable? I followed the advice I have given you in this book. I did some market research and tried out my new message to see how the market responded. I worked hard to mine my experience on how the motivational clichés didn't make sense in the real world. I verified that I could afford to make the shift and be okay financially before abandoning what was working. And then I stepped out. I made the decision that I was going to be the contrarian of the personal development industry. Doing that set me apart from the competition.

I threw away the suits. I put my earrings back in my ears—for years I had been taking them out for pictures and before going on stage. I started wearing cowboy shirts and cowboy boots. I became the Pitbull of Personal Development®. I trademarked that phrase, and I also trademarked, The World's Only *Irritational Speaker®*.

We all know what a motivational speaker is and the kinds of things they typically say. A motivational speaker will say something like, "Look, it's so beautiful over there. It's gorgeous. It's wonderful. Go over there, you'll love it. You will be happy and successful over there. Go!" That doesn't work for me and it won't work you either. At least long term it won't. I just don't believe that I can convince you that it's so nice over there that you are going to want to go from where you are to there. But what I am convinced of is that I can make you so irritated with where you are that you'll do anything to get away from it and go someplace else.

My approach is to make people so uncomfortable in their situation by proving to them that their decisions have created the mess they are living. Their finances, their relationships, their health and weight, their business is all the result of the way they think, the way they talk and because of their action. I remind them that they deserve, and can have better if they would change. I point out how painful it is to be where they are and get them moving in another direction. Any direction. I don't point out pretty places, I make them miserable with their current status. When it hurts where you are, you will go anyplace better.

People don't change because it's more comfortable someplace else regardless of how pretty some motivational speaker, success guru or thought leader promises them it will be. They change because it's so uncomfortable where they are that they can't stand being there even one more minute. I have spent thirty years perfecting the art of making people uncomfortable with where they were so they would eagerly go someplace else.

An aside about thought leaders. We hear a lot about thought leaders in the world today and we hear most of it from people who claim to be one. Here's what's funny about that: you don't get to proclaim yourself to be a thought leader. That's something that other people get to decide, not you. It is just one more bit of hyperbole and as far as I am concerned, arrogance. I've never professed to be a thought leader. Instead, I do profess to be an excellent thought follower. I have listened to the greatest speakers in the history of the world. I've read their words. The more you study the works of these great minds, the more you realize that many of them were just following the thoughts of other people who came before them. They only expanded on those great ideas and reframed them for a different time and a different audience.

I have never claimed to have had many original thoughts, but I have figured out an original way to express those thoughts.

Discover Your Uniqueness

Discover your uniqueness and learn to exploit it in the service of others and you are guaranteed success, happiness, and prosperity.

That's about the smartest thing I've ever said, so go back and read it again. That statement is the key to good marketing and to creating a competitive advantage. When you find your uniqueness and learn how to use it to serve customers well, you're pretty much there.

It's your job to figure out your uniqueness. I don't know what your uniqueness is, and I don't believe anyone can tell you what it is. I believe it is deeply rooted in who you are and your own personal story. It is based on your personal values and beliefs. It is grounded in your history. It takes work to uncover; but it's there.

My uniqueness is that I am more direct, blunt and to-the-point than other speakers. I have always been able to step on your toes and make you like it by being funny with my examples and stories. My goal has also been to be impossible to disagree with or to say "no" to. Pay attention to this part: *my goal has never been to be easy to say yes to or to agree with.* I want what I say to make so much sense that you can't figure out how to argue with me about it. You may not like it. You may hate what I have to say and you may hate me for saying it and that's fine.

But can you come up with a logical argument making my point incorrect?

My responsibility to you is to tell you the truth. You don't have to like the truth, but I am paid to tell you the truth—at least my interpretation of the truth.

As you read what I have written in this book about what it takes to be a successful entrepreneur, you might argue that you are going to be one of the exceptions to the statistics and facts about entrepreneurism. You are going to make it in ten years, be rich and happy, and nothing bad will ever happen along the way. No. The numbers just don't show that to be the case. Chances are, it's going to suck. Chances are, you're going to go out of business. Chances are, you're going to go broke and lose your savings and maybe your family and maybe your health. It's going to be horrible.

Am I a bad person for warning you of the truth? I can assure you that many will believe I am. You might be thinking that right now. But I believe I am serving you well by telling you the truth about the odds of your success and by helping you stack the deck in your favor.

Are you unique? Every single person who's reading this should be asking themselves: "How do I figure out a unique way to do what I do so that I stand out, and not competing based on price alone?"

As you're reading this, you may be thinking, "I run a dry cleaners. There are four dry cleaners in the same strip mall I'm in. I can't be the original." Not true. There is a way for you to be original or to be unique.

How do you figure out your uniqueness? You begin by spending some time on what isn't unique. Know what isn't unique and you are on your way to discovering what might be unique. The problem is that much of what people believe makes them unique isn't unique at all.

"We care about our customers." Big deal. That's a bare minimum and doesn't make you unique. Next?

"Location." Maybe, but probably not.

"Our people make us unique." Probably not. You have people, your competitors have people. You say your people are better and they say their people are better. What else you got? This is tougher than you thought isn't it!

"Our mission statement says we are passionate and dedicated to customer service and . . ." That's funny. Really, it's funny. Your mission statement—what you say about yourself and care about doesn't matter to much of anyone. They will never see it and you probably aren't living it like you think you are.

This is a tough exercise I have worked on with hundreds of companies. Most are simply clueless about what makes them unique and that's why they ultimately fail. When you are able to figure out what you offer that your customers can't get from anyone else and can demonstrate to your customers how that benefits them in tangible ways, your chances of being wildly successful go way up.

What does your business really do?

Another aspect of running a successful business is clarity of services. Know what your company does and be even more clear about what your company does not do. When you're starting a business, you have to say, "This is what I do. This is what I'm good at. This is how I can provide the most value to the marketplace. This is what makes me money."

Many companies start out saying, "I could do that. It's not exactly what I thought I could do but one person asked me for it so maybe I should do that too!" I could do a lot of things. I could do customer service training. I don't. I could do leadership training. I don't do that either. I get asked to do business consulting. Okay, but my definition of consulting is different than the definition used by other consultants. I coach businesses through many business issues but I'm not willing to do what it takes to be a Fortune 500 business consultant. Is it that I couldn't? No, it's that I have chosen not to. I say yes to what I am best at and no to things I could do that I would just be good at.

There are lots of things you could do, but that doesn't mean you should. You have to learn what to say no to.

When times are tough, people start saying yes to way too much. Some will say yes to almost everything simply because they need the money. I understand being flexible because you need the money. I've been broke before, too. But saying yes to things that are outside of what you are known for—and best at—is indeed a slippery slope. People water down their brands and diminish their reputation to the point they aren't known for anything. They have become the age-old cliché, jack-of-all-trades and master of none.

I see this a lot in the speaking industry. The other day a person asked me to take a look at his website and let him know what I thought. He listed seventy-two topics under his "areas of expertise."

I said, "You sure do a lot of topics."

He said, "Yes, I do. I'm really proud of the fact that I can talk about all of those things."

"That's a shame," I said, "because what most people are really looking for is time management." He had seventy-two topics but didn't have time management on his list.

"Oh, I could do time management."

"You missed my point," I said. "I'm not looking for you to add one more thing you can do. All speakers have something to say about most topics. But what are you best at talking about? What's the one thing that you can do better than anybody else so people will see you as the resource to contact on that topic?"

He didn't have a clue. He thought being able to talk about everything made him more desirable in the marketplace. I explained to him that just the opposite was true.

Many times, businesses fail not because of what they say yes to, but because they should be saying no to more things. If you say yes to everything, you're never going to be known for one thing. When you're known for one thing above all other things, that's when you can build a brand. That's when people will start to count on you for that one thing and pay you a premium for it.

Problems and Pain

You need to answer three questions before you can determine whether your business is viable: What problem does your business solve? What pain does it alleviate? Is the problem painful enough that people will spend money to solve it?

If you don't know the problem you are solving and don't know the cost or the pain that problem creates, then your solution is of little significance. Entrepreneurs all too often get too caught up in their solution and don't focus or understand the pain and the problem their customer is going through. People don't pay for solutions.

People pay to get rid of their problem and to stop feeling the pain.

Let's say you came to me and said, "Larry, this is my problem. It's killing my business. I don't know what to do about it. It's costing money. It's causing pain in my personal life and my professional life. I'm broke, and I'm behind on my taxes. I'll do anything, Larry, just tell me what to do."

If after listening to you, I told you to stand on your head in the corner and whistle The Star-Spangled Banner backwards, you would be over there in the corner right now, trying to figure out how to stand on your head. My solution wouldn't matter. If you believed I understood your problem and was able to identify with what you are going through and was connected to your pain, then you would do what I tell you to do to alleviate that pain. What the customer wants more than anything is for someone to understand the pain they are going through. The customer doesn't care about your solution; they want you to understand their pain. Forgetting this because you think your solution is so good can cost you everything.

People come to the marketplace with a solution without first determining whether there's a problem. In fact, I believe people are coming up with solutions to problems that don't even exist and then spend their time and money trying to convince the marketplace there is a problem.

You have to not only know the problem that exists, but you also have to know how that problem shows up in people's lives or businesses. You have to know what that problem costs them, both tangibly and intangibly. What is the emotional cost of having the problem? When you know what the problem is costing someone then you can figure out what they are willing to pay for it.

The winning formula

Find a problem that exists in the world today, then determine what it costs people to experience that problem. That is the pain of having the problem. Figure out the costs of having that pain and then figure out how your solution alleviates the pain.

The difference between the solution and the pain tends to confuse people. Let's use Pepto-Bismol as an example: Pepto-Bismol doesn't approach the marketplace by saying, "Here is this pink, chalky liquid that will turn your tongue black and is kind of hard to get down. We have also turned it into gum and pills, but they don't work as well as the liquid stuff. You want it? It will make your tummy feel better!" Pepto-Bismol is a fine solution but nobody is going to buy the solution I just described.

If they don't sell the solution, what do they sell instead? They sell the problem and the pain: nausea, heartburn, indigestion, upset stomach, diarrhea. They create commercials that talk about the pain and make a little jingle and dance to drive the pain home. Chances are you can sing the song and dance the dance right now. They don't sell pink, chalky stuff that tastes yucky and turns your tongue black. They sell getting rid of nausea, heartburn, indigestion, upset stomach, diarrhea. And if you have any of those things, they know you are willing to do whatever it takes to get rid of them.

How about your product or service? Are you selling the pink, chalky solution? Or are you connecting around the heartburn and indigestion? Start selling to the pain that people are experiencing because if you don't understand their pain, can't remind them of the pain, and can't make them feel that pain, then you can't make the sale.

The sale is always based on your understanding of the customer's problem and not their understanding of your solution.

What is it worth? What will you charge for your product or service? You determine your pricing based on the size, quantity, and cost of the problem you solve. If your solution costs $12 and the problem is a $10 problem, then it's cheaper to have the problem than it is to pay for the solution. Who is going to spend money on a solution that costs more than the problem it solves? Not many. Your job, as an entrepreneur with a product or service to sell, is to do the cost analysis for the customer so they can see and feel that your solution costs less than the cost of what they are going through.

In order to have a successful company, the customer must see your solution as having value to them. And the value is not only what it does for them but the cost of what you do for them makes sense from a money standpoint. They have to feel like they are getting their money's worth. They are not going to spend a hundred dollars on a fifty-dollar problem. You have a couple of choices to make. You can help them understand that their fifty-dollar problem carries other costs that actually end up making the cost of their problem much more than fifty dollars. Or you can lower the price of your solution to be less than fifty dollars. How does that sound? Sounds pretty awful, doesn't it? You have to lower your price and give up your profitability all because you can't justify the cost to the customer. You fail to understand their problem, their pain and what that problem and pain is costing them. Message? Do your homework. Know in advance what the problem you solve costs people, then price your product or service so it appears to be a bargain in the mind of the customer.

It costs a few hundred bucks to get your chimney cleaned. The cost of a housefire because you didn't do it?

It costs fifty bucks to get your oil changed. The cost of repairing your care engine when you don't do it?

See how it works? Sell the pain of not taking advantage of the solution.

The Customer Experience

Much is said today about creating a great customer experience. In fact, it's talked about so much that it has been reduced from Customer Experience to CX—another buzzword to keep up with that just means making sure the customer is happy when they finish doing business. There are books and courses and seminars and videos and audios all about how to do it. The idea has been around since the first product was sold, and people have been trying to perfect it forever. Here's my take on the customer experience: they always have one. It might be a good one or a bad one. Maybe one so insignificant they won't even remember it. Maybe it will be one so amazing they will never forget it. Maybe it will be so horrible they will tell everyone about it. But regardless of the kind they have, they will still have one. It is your job to create the kind of experience they have that will positively reflect on you and your company.

For too many, creating a great customer experience has become a little silly. We've tried to make the experience so amazing that the main goal of the product and service has gotten lost along the way. I have had people work so hard at making me happy in order to give me an amazing customer service experience that I've lost my willingness to do business with them. I don't want to put up with the rigmarole of going through their antics. Sometimes it's, "I just came here to get a sandwich; make this easy for me."

We have to understand that not all customers are looking for the same experience. For instance, if I want a pizza, I don't go to Chuck E. Cheese because I don't want the experience of the little kids and the stuffed rat playing the cymbals. I'm looking for a different experience, so I get pizza from a different place.

How do you know the customer experience you are providing is a good one? Are your customers coming back for more? If they're not coming back—if it was a one and done—then customer experience was probably not all that good. Duh!

So what are you doing that brings people back over and over again? I have a philosophy about selling that flows over into business: find out what the customer wants and give them more of it; then find out what they don't want and don't give them any of that. Do that with your customers. Ask them what you are doing that brings them back. It's that easy!

Recently I had a conversation with my buddy Scott McKain, author of *Iconic: How Organizations and Leaders Attain, Sustain and Regain The Ultimate Level of Distinction*. Scott is constantly doing research on standing out in the marketplace and delivering the ultimate customer experience. In fact, he even owns the trademark, The Ultimate Customer Experience® so he knows this subject like no one else. What Scott told me about what people value most in an experience might surprise you. He told me that what people want most is to feel like somebody is being nice to them. Customers value friendliness more than ever before.

What does it cost to be friendly? Really, what's the expense? Where do you put friendliness on your expense sheet? It doesn't cost you anything to be friendly. For many years, my whole message about customer service has been simple: just be nice. It turns out people value that. They want to have an experience of a friendly environment. If that's what people want, and Scott and I both believe it is, then I would do everything in my power to make sure that happens.

We make it all so hard. It turns out that one of the top ways you can get a competitive edge is by being nice to people and that costs you nothing.

I like to go to Waffle House. I like the breakfast for sure. But one of the other reasons I like going there is because when I walk in, the whole staff looks up and says, "Good morning, welcome to Waffle House!" In all honesty, I don't really care whether they mean it or not; I just feel so much better that they said it and that they act like they are glad to see me. It's really easy to create a good customer experience.

We typically think it has to do with bells and whistles and doing crazy, unique stuff and it just doesn't. Customers want you to be friendly. They want you to be nice to them and treat them with appreciation. They want consistency. They want doing business with you to make sense from a pricing standpoint. They want your product or your service to cost less than the problem they're going through. That's all they're looking for. It doesn't take that much to do it. When you're building your business, you have to keep those things in mind. It's about serving people well with your product and service and making them see that it's a cheaper solution for them than living with the problem and the pain that they're going through.

In other words, you show them that you care about what they're going through. That's when you build enough trust that people will share their money with you. The great speaker, author and entrepreneur Earl Nightingale said, "All of the money you are ever going to have is currently in the hands of someone else." I have never forgotten that great line since the first time I heard it nearly forty years ago.

In business, that "someone else" Earl is referring to is called the customer. The way to get the customer to share their money with you is to solve their problem and alleviate their pain. Make sure that the cost of your solution is less than the cost of their problem. Do it in a nice, friendly, appreciative way. It's that simple. Entrepreneurs have so much to focus on when it comes to being successful, but this is a basic that requires your attention every second of every day. The customer has the money that keeps you in business. You can't be too nice them.

Beating the competition

There's a lot of talk in business circles about beating the competition. Most companies tend to get very defensive about how much better they are. But *you* don't get to determine whether or not you're better than the competition. Your vote doesn't count. The marketplace always decides. Always. My buddy, Joe Calloway, author of *Be The Best At What Matters Most* and many other great books is like a broken record on this fact. I will often say about a certain coffee chain, "Their coffee sucks!" And he will always respond with, "Well, the market doesn't think so Larry, because their stock price is at an all-time high, they typically have huge lines out the door, and other customers think their coffee tastes great. The market has decided you are wrong, Larry. The market decides, not you." Yep, Joe is correct. I'm wrong. Their coffee doesn't suck. How do I know that? The market has decided that it doesn't. Their coffee doesn't appeal to me, but I am in the minority according to the marketplace.

So what you have to say about how great you are compared to your competition doesn't matter. What is the market saying? The market decides who wins and who loses, not you.

If a certain factor about the way you do business doesn't matter to a certain customer, then it just doesn't matter to that customer. It doesn't matter whether you think it should or not. That customer doesn't care. If that customer doesn't care about what you think should matter to them, where does that leave you? It leaves you without them as your customer. It doesn't matter if you are better than your competition if the customer doesn't care.

Trying to be all things to all customers is a fast path to failure. You have to understand your target market. *Better* is a relative term. You have to create such uniqueness about how you do what you do that the competition becomes almost irrelevant.

A few years ago, a friend of mine in the speaking business told me about a conversation he had with a new speaker who called him and said, "I don't understand. I see what Winget does and what Winget charges. I see what you do and what you charge. Then I look at what I do and what I charge. I don't get it. Why does Winget charge so much more money we do?"

My friend explained it to him this way: "Here's what you don't understand. There are a thousand of you. There might be ten of me. There's only one Winget."

When the customer recognizes what you do and values what you do and see you as the only option for getting what you do, you can charge a premium for doing what you do. That was always my goal.

I contend that everybody can discover their uniqueness. It's not easy. I would remind you again of this: You rarely know what your uniqueness is, but you always know what it isn't. Focus on what *isn't* unique about you and downplay that since everyone else is probably already doing that. You are chasing your tail trying to be like everybody else. Being like everybody else won't get you paid much, because the customer can just as easily go to someone else as they can to you.

Delivering Your Product

Your business exists to be profitable. It is profitable because your business expenses are lower than your cost of doing business. You have a business because you have figured out a way to add value to the lives or businesses of others. You price your value so it costs less to purchase your value (solution) than it does for the customer (recipient of that value) to have the problem.

These things never change. They are inflexible. However, how you do these things might change. In fact, I believe it likely that they will change.

I have been getting on airplanes to travel to meetings to do speeches in front of audiences for over thirty years. And all of that changed in 2020. I was no longer able to travel and there were no longer large groups of people gathering for meetings. My product, service and value did not change; however the way I delivered my product, service and value have changed dramatically.

That might have been the case for your business during the pandemic as well. Many businesses changed the way they provided their products and services to their customers. Those who figured out how to do it probably survived. They might not have thrived, but their flexibility allowed them to survive. Those who were unable to be flexible in providing their products and services, probably went out of business.

Something is always going to change about the way you do business. Hopefully it won't be a global pandemic—but something is still going to change, and you are going to have to be flexible in how you deliver your products and services.

Technology is going to change the way you do business. We all used to read books only printed on paper. Chances are high that you are reading this book on a device and not turning pages on a physical book. I get it if you are turning pages, as I like to read business books that way as well.

We used to go into brick-and-mortar stores to buy clothes and chances are you now order most of your clothes online or from an app.

I buy most of my groceries from an app now as well as almost every other thing I buy. These changes are something we could not have imagined just a few years ago but now take for granted. Can you prepare for the rapid change in technology? Only if you are flexible in your thinking and open to change. Stop being open to change and you might as well shut the doors today— because you are not going to make it.

Times change things. Everything moves from the way it's being done today to the way it will be done in the future. It requires great flexibility in how you do business. And that is going to come down to willingness. You know examples right now of how people were unwilling and inflexible and refused to change the way they did business. Those people are, more than likely, out of business.

Addressing a niche

Many businesses have a generic approach to solving problems. That approach is mostly built on doing business *my* way, with you buying *my* solution, *my* product and *my* service the way I want to sell it. If you're lucky, it might apply to the way you want to buy it. Good luck with that. You have to meet people where they are and not where you want them to be. You have to sell to people the way they want to buy.

You can personalize your product and service simply by understanding what your customers are going through.

I do a lot of dry cleaning. I seem to go to the dry cleaners all the time. I like my shirts done a certain way. I like my jeans to have heavy starch. I like so much starch you can't put your foot through the legs because they are stuck together, and you almost need a pry-bar to get the legs opened up for your feet to go through. It's called cowboy starch. Dry cleaners can compete based on many factors. They can compete based on price. They can compete based on convenience. They can compete based on service and a lot of different things.

There are several dry cleaners in the same little shopping center where I go. One is a bargain dry cleaner. One is a speed cleaner. One brags about their service. But do you know why I picked the one I go to? Easy parking. It has four spots in front, designated just for them and there's a ten-minute limit on how long you can park there. I would never go where I'd have to park all the way across the lot, drag my bag full of dirty clothes in, and tell them how to do my shirts and jeans. That's way more effort than I am willing to invest. I go to my dry cleaners because the parking is easy. The dry cleaning is all pretty much the same and the cost and speed differential is minimal. I could go to any of the dry cleaners, and my shirts and jeans would look pretty much the same. But the effort isn't worth it to me. I want convenient parking.

The quality—the product—doesn't change, but they cater to the guy who's in a hurry and doesn't want the hassle of looking for a parking place. It wouldn't matter if I parked across the parking lot if I had all day long to do this stuff. Like most people I probably need the exercise. But because I don't want to fool with any of it, I go to the place where I can get in and out the fastest.

Maybe this dry cleaner had that in mind when they spent the money to reserve those four spots and put up the signage about the ten-minute limit, or maybe they lucked into it. But I know that every time I go to that dry cleaner there is a spot right at the front door and I think to myself, "This is great!"

You can customize your product or service and make the client feel it was meant just for them by understanding who they are, what they're going through, and how it differs from your competition. The people who value that will do business with you and will possibly, even probably, pay a premium for what they value.

4

Why Most Small Businesses Fail

I'm the Pitbull of Personal Development® because pit-
bulls are known for grabbing onto something, locking
their jaws, and not letting go. Similarly, if you're going
to be a successful entrepreneur, you have to lock on and
not let go. People fail because they let go of things and let
the things that matter slip away from them. When that
happens their business gets out of control, and they don't
last. In ten years, no one will have ever heard of them and
the entrepreneur is working a day job and probably still
paying off the debt of their failed venture.

Let's talk about some of the reasons people fail
when they start their own businesses. I've done a lot
of research on this subject and I could write for a long
time about why businesses fail, as the reasons are so

plentiful. But there are a few big ones to make sure you understand.

Deliver value

According to entrepreneur.com, the number one reason businesses fail is that they fail to deliver real value. As I've said, people honestly believe when they start their business that they are offering value but they're offering value from their own point of view, not from the point of view of the customer or the marketplace. They see their own value, but they have failed to communicate it in such a way that anybody who does business with them will pay money for it.

You must constantly be adding value. What kind of value? Tangible value. Tangible means measurable. Does it make me more money or help me sell more? Does it help me hire better employees? Does it help me spend less money? Does it help me be a better leader or manager? Does it help me serve my customers better? All of these are tangible things that can be measured and that people will immediately see the value in.

There is also intangible value. How does it make me feel? Does it make me feel better about who I am? Does it make me feel better about my relationships? Does it reduce anxiety or stress? Does it allow me to worry less? Smoke less? Drink less? Get angry less? Yell less? Does it help me sleep better at night? (That's a valuable tangible and non-tangible!) Sometimes those intangibles are just as important as the tangibles.

At any rate, that's how your value will be determined. Your value is determined through the eyes of the customer and not just through your own eyes. What you believe doesn't really matter. It's always what you're able to get your customers to believe about their situation. They determine the value of your product, which determines your price, which determines how much money you will earn.

Just Say No

I coach a lot of people on how to write books. I always begin by asking, "Who is this book for?" People will often say, "It's for everybody." That's a lousy answer. Whatever it is you offer in terms of products or services can't be for everybody. Could everybody use it? Possibly. Will everybody use it? Absolutely not. So target as specifically as you can. Figure out who your product or service will serve in the best way. You know how you determine that? By determining whom your product and service is *not* for.

I wrote a book entitled *Your Kids Are Your Own Fault: A Guide For Raising Responsible, Productive Adults.* In order for me to figure out my target market the book was specifically intended for, I got very clear with what kind of a parenting book this wasn't. This book was not for parents with babies who want to learn how to change diapers or feed their baby and keep it healthy. My book was specifically written for parents who want to know how to create responsible, productive adults. I was writing to people about how they could raise their children with the skills and core values to be responsible and productive as they move into adulthood. I don't believe we raise children; I believe we create adults. So, I got very clear about what my book *wasn't* in order to be clear about what it was.

You have to be clear about what your business *isn't* in order to be clear about what your business *is*. You have to be clear about whom your business is not for, so you won't waste your time, energy, and money trying to sell to people who are not your target market. Why are you talking to those people who are not the ones you really want to be your customer? Sell to the people who are the prime prospects for your product or service. Know your market.

I worked with a coaching client recently who just wasn't closing enough sales. She would spend most of her day talking to clients in her sales funnel but when the program was explained to them and she asked them to buy, very few were saying yes. The problem wasn't leads as she had plenty of leads. After I looked at her marketing materials and her messaging on her website and social media, it was obvious that her appeal was so broad that everyone felt they could benefit from talking to her. Sounds good on the surface but it turned out that was her problem. Everyone qualified themselves as a prospect for her services. Most of them didn't have any money or any intention of fixing their issues; they just wanted to know more about her services. So her day was filled with people talking to her about what she did, but not buying. She had done a great job of identifying the pain in people's lives. They felt the pain and wanted her service, but she hadn't made it clear that in order to do business with her, there was a serious commitment of time and money involved. We reworked her marketing materials to make it clear that while many people had the problem she was able to help them with, she only worked with people who earned at a certain level, had a business of a certain size, and were willing to commit a certain amount of time. She disqualified the people who were taking up her time through her messaging, so they didn't waste her time in the actual sales process. That gave her fewer people to talk to for sure. But the people she ended up with weren't shoppers or tire-kickers, they were true prospective buyers. As a result of this shift to making it clear who her services were not for, she ended up with more time and more clients.

Disciplined growth

It will be natural for you to want to grow and expand your business into new areas. I am all for growth and expansion unless it takes your focus off of your core business. If you lose focus on your core business—the thing that keeps the steady flow of revenue coming in—then you are going to find yourself in trouble pretty quickly. If you get distracted and start to pursue more exciting avenues simply because you are a little bored with what you have been doing, then your core customers are going to suffer and look elsewhere for service. When you lose your core business, which is the primary source of your revenue, you are at risk of losing everything.

I recently did an interview with David Morris, who owns Dillanos Coffee Roasters of Seattle, Washington. His is a fabulous story of an entrepreneur who figured out how to become a major player in the coffee business. Although you are probably unaware of ever drinking Dillanos Coffee, you probably have since it is marketed under so many different private labels.

David and I spoke about so many entrepreneurs distracted by looking at the things they can do but probably shouldn't do. He told me that he was very tempted to become a coffee retailer but realized that being in the retail coffee business is entirely different from being in the wholesale coffee processing business and that it would be smarter and more profitable to stick with what he was best at. He told me several stories of the different opportunities he had learned the hard way *not* to participate in because they took his focus off his core business. He said, "Every investment I ever made that was outside of my core area of interest and expertise failed. They all failed because my fortune has been made doing this, just this, and nobody is better at doing this than I am."

I thought to myself, that idea reinforces so much about my own business success.

When I show up to give a speech—online, or in person—nobody does it quite like I do it. If a client isn't looking for exactly what I do, and the way I do it, they should hire somebody else. My core business is doing keynote speeches. That's what I do. That's what I built my company and reputation on. The spin off of my core business is converting speeches to audio and video programs as well as to books. These products are just extensions of my core business, but they're not an entirely different business.

If I started doing events or running a bureau for speakers, chances are high that I would either fail at the new venture or my speaking business would fail because I would be splitting my focus. Over the years many people have asked me to become involved in various ventures related to being in the speaking industry. Every time I've been tempted and succumbed, it hasn't worked out for me. Something always suffered and typically, it was my core business. I ventured into things that were related, interesting and fun to do, but were not the primary source of my revenue and not what I was best at. I have learned over the years to say no to just about everything that doesn't have keynote speaking at the foundation.

> Success comes as much from saying no
> as it does from saying yes.

Stay focused on what you do that makes you the most amount of money. That idea will serve you well for the rest of your life as an entrepreneur. Learn to get good at saying no to things that distract you. If a new opportunity distracts you to the point of obsession, then sell the business you've got and start a new one, but don't undermine the success of your current business. Don't become distracted to the point where your business starts to suffer all because one more shiny object has shown up in your life and you can't turn your head away from it.

Control Your Expenses

The next big reason that entrepreneurs fail has to do with how they spend their money. When you lose control of your expenses, you've lost control of your business. It's that black-and-white. And it can happen in the blink of eye. Your expenses will get out of control very quickly if you are easily distracted.

If these things sound like you, you are going to have expense-control issues:

"Ooh, I need to redo my website again."
"Ooh, ooh, ooh, I need to go that seminar across the country."
"Ooh, I need to hire a new coach."
"Ooh, I need to get a new service truck."

You must constantly be focused on your bottom line. Your bottom line includes both your revenue as well as your expenses. And your expenses have elements that seem so insignificant they can easily be ignored and allow you to say to yourself, "That's no big deal." Never kid yourself, every expense is a big deal and must be treated as if it is.

Your expenses can get away from you one $12 per month subscription at a time. I've seen it happen many times when working with entrepreneurs. A $12 subscription here and a $17 subscription there and before you know it, hundreds of dollars are being charged every single month. A few hundred a month ends up a few thousand a year. That's money you could easily have used to pay toward something more revenue-generating or maybe even to pay yourself!

Be careful of your numbers and control your expenses. Chances are you do not need to hire somebody. Chances are you can suck it up and work a little harder all by yourself before you add the expense of another employee. Chances are you can live another month without whatever it is you think is a need when it's just another shiny object.

Wants, Needs and Can't-Live-Withouts

If you have ever read much about handling money, you are familiar with the idea of dividing expenses into wants and needs. Okay, I'm fine with that. But I find this isn't quite enough to get people thinking as they should if they are ever going to be success entrepreneurs and run a profitable business. You have to consider what you need. You have to play with the idea of the things you want. But if you really want to control expenses you must get real about what you can't live without.

You need to pay your commitments. Your commitments are your bills. A deal is a deal. You made a deal with your credit card company to pay them a certain amount on a certain day every month. You even signed a contract. You need to pay it. It's a matter of integrity. Besides, you want people to pay you, don't you? Of course you do. Remember this: Money comes to you as it goes from you. If you don't pay your bills as you agreed to, then don't be surprised when others don't pay you. That's the way it works.

So number one, you need to pay your commitments.

The next category: wants. The bottom line on this one is just because you want it, doesn't mean you need it. I want a lot of things I simply don't need. You do, too. It's natural and even healthy to want more than you have—unless wanting it causes you to give in to buying it, and you end up spending money you don't have to get it.

Need some help with being able to decipher the difference between a need and a want? Move it into my next category: Can't live without it.

You can live without a lot of things. More than you think you can. In fact, you can live just fine without most of what you think of as a necessity. As a human being you can't live without food, water and shelter. In your business you can't live without customers and a product or service plus a delivery method for your product and service. What can't you live without to have customers? A website, an email account, and a phone. No way around those in today's world. Customers have to be able to figure out who you are and what you do, and they have to be able to contact you and have you contact them. You can't survive without those things.

There are other things you can't live without when it comes to your business and many of those things are determined by the kind of business you run. But I will guarantee you it takes less than you think. It's time right now for you to take a good, hard look at your expenses and begin thinking of each line item as a need, a want or a can't-live-without. Be honest with yourself. It's a tough exercise for sure but one that just might keep you in business!

When it's all your own money

Some of the entrepreneurs who are the best at controlling their expenses are those who have had to fund their business with only their own capital. This is often called bootstrapping. I'm not saying that bootstrapping is the best idea for everybody starting a business, but I like it because it makes you think harder before you spend money. It makes you more conservative in your spending for sure. It makes you smarter about what you buy and when you buy it. It makes you pay more attention to your numbers, and you always have to pay attention to your numbers. Your numbers are everything. The numbers are your boss. (Remember that?) When it's your money at stake every single day, you pay more attention.

We can all become a little sloppy and lazy when somebody else's money is financing us. Regardless of what we do today, their money will probably be there tomorrow. When it's our very own money, and it might not be there tomorrow, we tend to do whatever it takes to keep adding profitability to the bottom line.

I think it's fine to incur a certain amount of debt. I'm not one of those anti-debt personal finance guys. Debt can be a very good thing when used and managed properly. You just have to make sure you can make your payments on the debt. If your debt gets to the point where you can't service the debt by making the payments, then you can't survive. There is an old saying we should all remember: "When your outgo exceeds your income, then your upkeep becomes your downfall."

When it comes to using someone else's money, avoid family money when at all possible. If you borrow from your parents or siblings and can't repay the money, then you have not only lost your business, but maybe your family as well. It's not worth it. And remember that when you borrow from family, their nose is going to be in your business. You might not think that's fair. You probably won't like when they ask you about what you are doing, or your judgment or what you are spending money on, but being your financier comes at a price. Their nose in your business is that price.

I see people making another mistake when it comes to debt: they put their own family's future at stake. As I've already pointed out, a certain amount of risk is always involved in starting your own business. If you are totally risk-averse, you shouldn't even think about becoming an entrepreneur. But you've got to be really careful if you are risking your family's financial future for you to follow your dream. My suggestion is that you always put your family and their security first. You can go into a reasonable amount of indebtedness when you are absolutely confident that you are able to pay off the debt. If there is any doubt about that, then don't go into debt.

I also like the idea of people bootstrapping their own dream, because it's their dream and not someone else's. I like the idea of people using their money for their dream, their plan and their business.

On a personal level, I don't want to be beholden to anybody. I don't want them to have a say in what I do, what I spend, what I market, or how I market it. I don't want to give up that level of control. And the one who has the money has the control. If you're using someone else's money, that person will eventually exert their power over that money. If there is any way to start your business with just your own money, do it. Yes, the process might be slower. Yes, you won't grow as fast. Yes, it's going to take you longer. But if you fail it's on you, and if you succeed it's on you.

If-Then Logic

Of course, you have to have a strategic plan for the way your business should work at every level. But you also have to have a strategic plan for what happens when that plan doesn't work. You must have some processes and some systems outlined so that you can say, "when this happens, this is how my company responds" or "when this bad thing happens, I'm going to do that."

When I was in college, I learned about if-then logic: "If this happens, then this happens."

That's what I'm asking you to use in your business. Figure out what is supposed to happen within some area of your business. Write down some scenarios that illustrate "when we get in this situation, I will do these things." You need a sales process, customer service process, product delivery, collections and more. And never think that you get by without having these things written down. You can't. Always work from document, not from thought.

I'm not going to go into a lot of detailed business plan stuff here. There are many books written on how to write a business plan by people who are better at it than I am. But I am going to be very clear that you need a structural process for how you do things and how you run your business. That structural process is based on, "when this happens, this happens." You need both a proactive process and a reactive process. A plan for what happens when things go right, and a plan for what happens when things go wrong. Businesses without anything written down on paper, who work only from emotion, thought and memory, will fail. Figure out all of this in advance.

That is the essence of what you have to know in order to be in business. If you've hung with me this far, then you're ready to figure out how to put your business together so you can succeed. Things like how you can be a good leader, how you can build your company, and how to sell and serve other people better. Then I'll talk to you about what to do when it all goes to hell.

5

When You Go It All By Yourself

For a lot of people, starting their own business conjures up images of people like Jeff Bezos or Steve Jobs. Entrepreneurs see their garage or their kitchen table and imagine complex businesses with hundreds and thousands of employees, investors, huge budgets, big buildings, and more.

While that can happen, the reality of entrepreneurship for most is quite different. The vast majority of businesses are small businesses. In fact, they are very, very small businesses. According to the small-business website thebalance.com, 73% of all businesses in America are sole proprietorships. Solopreneurship is a natural way for people to get into business all on their own, away from their nine-to-five jobs.

A stream-lined process

For me, the advantage of solopreneurship is primarily that you are in it by yourself. When someone tells me about their dreams of a thousand employees, that seems like nothing but a nightmare to me.

One of the biggest downsides of a big company, or even a small one with more than one employee, is how complicated it is to get something done. In fact, to get anything done! When you are all by yourself, you get away from all having to involve so many people in making decisions. Layers of decision making is just a headache for most people who truly have an entrepreneurial spirit. Entrepreneurs want the speed that comes from doing the job by themselves, or at most, with a very small team of employees they direct. They want to be able to make decisions quickly and turn their business on a dime. That can't be done in most small businesses and it certainly can't be done in a really large business.

Of course, while the advantages of being in it all by yourself are many, there are disadvantages.

Whose fault is it?

The first big disadvantage that comes to mind is that you don't have anybody else to blame. We're a society that loves to blame someone else. We love to blame our coworkers.

Walk into any business in America with a complaint, and the first thing you will probably hear is, "It's not my fault. It's their fault." Complain to the salesperson and they will blame the customer service department. Then the customer service department will blame installation or manufacturing. Before you know it, it was the janitor's fault. Bosses blame their employees and employees blame the boss. And the list goes on and on and on. We are a society that thrives on blame and a lack of responsibility.

As a solopreneur, you've got no place to lay the blame except to the mirror. If it was done wrong, it was your fault. And because we don't teach personal responsibility much anymore, most people are not able to accept the blame themselves. They can't handle not having someone else to blame or to lay fault on. That's why many people simply don't fit the solopreneur mold and will never be happy going it alone. They don't want to be the one who's chewed out when it's done wrong. Like most, they love getting all the credit when it's done right, but they want none of the blame when it's done wrong. People who are not conditioned to accept responsibility for all of it should keep their day job.

Decide already!

Decision making is also an issue for most people, making solopreneurship a challenge. Most people don't understand the decision making process and aren't very good at it. Again, we are not taught how to make good decisions or what to do when we make bad decisions. People are used to decision by committee or focus group. When they are faced with, "What should I do?" their first reaction is, "What would you do?" They want the comfort that comes from making a decision supported by a group of people or a team. Or better yet, they want someone to make the decision for them and then they will implement the other person's decision. This kind of person needs a company and a boss. They do not need to start their own company or be their own boss.

When you are your own boss, you are making decisions all day long. And you have to be able to make them fast and live with the decision you have made. Most people think every decision they make has to be a good one. I can assure you that most of the good decisions I have made in my life have been the result of education I received from making really bad decisions. If you are not willing to make a lot of bad decisions and try a lot of stuff that doesn't work, you're never going to have confidence in your ability to make decisions.

The sheer quantity of decisions can be overwhelming sometimes, and as a solopreneur you're the only one who gets to make them. Some people just aren't equipped for that. You've got to realize, "I'm the only one who is to blame for this, and I'm the one who's got to make all of the decisions." That's tough.

Here is my advice for decision making: "Make the decision, then make the decision right." If you are paralyzed by the thought of making the right decision because you are so afraid that you will make the wrong decision, follow this advice. Know the upside and the downside of making the decision. In other words, understand the consequences before you decide. But then, just decide. Make the decision. Then do everything in your power to make sure that the decision you just made was the right one. No second guessing. That's counterproductive. No whining. No, "I wish I had . . ." Just make the decision and put all of your energy into making whatever you decided work out. Make the decision, then make the decision right. Will all of your decisions be right? Ha. Absolutely not. That comes with the territory. Deal with it.

Money issues again

Many solopreneurs only have their own money to work with. They have just enough money to buy enough product to get started or to create a website so they can start a coaching business, or whatever it is they have decided to do. The bottom line for most entrepreneurs who strike out on their own is that they are undercapitalized from the get-go. They don't have very deep pockets. Ideally, before you get started, you've got to have deep enough pockets to cover your expenses for six months minimum. Most people don't have that, as our society simply hasn't taught us to save money. When you start your business undercapitalized with no reserves to carry you at all, you are starting with one foot in the grave. You have a dream, a new business, little money, little experience and no one to blame but yourself. You're in a tough spot.

Discipline Is The Key

Discipline is the key personality trait required for being a solopreneur. You must be able to get up in the morning and go into a dedicated workspace where you can block yourself off from the rest of your family and your world. Then you have to focus on adding value to the customers you have, while making sure your message attracts more customers. You have to deliver your products and services as you promised you would. You have to deal with interruptions, distractions and the occasional full-blown crisis. And you have to do all of this while making sure you are profitable. Then you have to do it all again tomorrow. And the next day. And the next day after that. It never ends. To accomplish this Herculean effort, you must be disciplined.

Remember, that your number one priority is to take care of the revenue. Run out of revenue and you're out of business, so never stop taking your focus off of revenue and profitability. Most people don't have that level of discipline as they are distracted by their passion for being in business on their own. Stick with that passion and let me know how that works out for you. The rest of you, the ones of you who focus on profitability, send me a thank you and buy me a bottle of bourbon for being a broken record on this stuff.

The absolute truth about way too many people with a nine-to-five job is they are used to doing just enough to keep from getting fired by their employer. In fact, it's one of the reasons they wanted to start their own business. Bad employees who can't work for someone else decide they want to go out on their own. You can't get along with anyone, so the solution is to quit your job, give up your steady paycheck and become a solopreneur. Brilliant idea! When you aren't willing to change you, just change your situation. That always works, right?

Your level of discipline has to be extreme so you can get up in the morning whether you feel like it or not, and hit the bricks running. When you have a nine-to-five job, you have sick leave. If you are a solopreneur and you're sick your business is closed—but probably not. You can't close your business because you have the sniffles. You struggle through it because there isn't anyone else to do the work. You don't get sick leave when you're all in it by yourself. You also don't have health insurance unless you're willing to pay for it. And you should be willing to pay for it! There are a lot of perks that come with being employed by a company that go away once you are in it all by yourself. Every single day, you've got to get up with the discipline that enables you to keep at it when you don't feel like it, when you hate it, and when you're sick of the very thought of it. You hate looking at your desk, you hate your customers, you hate your computer, you hate just thinking of doing one more Zoom call and guess what? You still have commitments, so you do it all anyway. That's discipline. If there is any hesitancy with that idea, bail out now and save yourself the grief and disappointment. That's what being a solo-preneur is all about.

Suck it up, Buttercup

In addition to discipline, you also need to develop really thick skin so that you're able to shrug the crappy stuff off and keep going. You are going to hear "no" and experience disappointment more than you ever dreamed of. Things are not going to work out. Other people's opinions don't have much to do with you. You've got to keep your head down and stay focused. Have the discipline to keep going even when the world is being really nasty to you.

You are going to get bad Yelp reviews. People will say things online that are totally unfair and are probably flat out lies about you. Personally, I have had death threats and get horrible emails from people saying things I can't imagine saying to another human being. That's just part of the deal. If you can't handle the ugliness that comes with the deal, then don't do this. You have to be able to dust yourself off and move on when things aren't going well; and things aren't going to go well. You still have to get up every single day, experience the failure, experience the setbacks, dust yourself off, and move on down the road. If you stop, you fall behind.

Know When to Quit

A good entrepreneur knows that when something is not working, they need to stop doing it. Some folks have such a high level of stick-to-it-ness that they don't know when to quit.

Entrepreneurs love to say, "Failure is not an option." Bull. Failure is always an option. In fact, when you start your own business, failure is probable so don't let your emotions convince you otherwise. Attitude is important for sure, but attitude doesn't pay the bills. That is another reason for you to watch revenue and profitability. If it's not making you any money, that's a clue that maybe you ought to do something else.

Here is another stupid entrepreneurial cliché that I hear way too often: "People just give up too quickly." No, actually, people don't give up quickly enough. One of the dumbest things ever said was, "Never give up!" Wrong. There is a time to give up. When nothing you are doing is working, give up. Don't go broke on the hope it will work. Hope is not a strategy for success. There is no shame in giving up one thing to save another thing. If you have to give up on your passionate dream to save your family or your house or your sanity, then give up! Give up willingly and with dignity.

How about this little cliché of idiocy: "Winners never quit." Seriously? Winners quit all the time. The fact is that true winners know when to quit. To be successful, you have to know when to quit. If something isn't working, quit. If it's the wrong path, get off that path and take another path.

There is a time to quit and there is a time to stay. There is a time to give up and a time to double-down. Some people are so bullheaded that they will stick with their business and go down with the ship when the lifeboat was right there in front of them. They'll take their family down, their friends down, their friends' money down, and their family's money down. It will all go underwater simply because they're pigheaded. That kind of thinking is pure arrogance.

Back to the numbers again. You have to constantly go back to your numbers. If it's adding revenue to your bottom line, it's a good activity. If it's not—assess, assess, assess. Look at your situation every single day. Ask yourself what you can do differently? Could you tweak it a little bit? Is there a way to change it up so it adds more value? Could I change my messaging so I can communicate my benefits more clearly or make them feel their pain more so they will want to do business with me? Many times, it's not quitting everything, it's only quitting one thing that isn't working as part of the overall process. It's not always about giving it all up, but about giving something up.

Which Business to Start?

Some people are so intrigued by solopreneurship and the perceived freedom and independence that it supposedly brings that they want to start a business with little or no clue of what kind to start. While that is amazing to me, I know it's not all that uncommon. I suggest that the best thing is a business that suits the skills you already have. When I decided to become a speaker, I was already really good at selling. I had experience selling from the time I was very young. I had been a professional salesperson and won sales awards. I had read every book on selling I could find. So, I had my content and I knew what I could speak about. I had also written sales training and taught it in my previous jobs. It was not a brand-new skill set for me. I had the advantage of both experience and research.

Sales training was not my passion. I didn't love it. But I was good at it. I have made this point already many times: people pay for your value, not your passion. I brought tangible value to the marketplace. I knew that well in advance of beginning my new business. I was prepared.

Don't start a business where you have no experience or haven't done your research. This is not the time to gamble with your future while you go out and try to figure out how to do something new. The best business for you is the one you know you can make money doing. Have the knowledge. Have the skills. Have some basic talent. But most of all, have the ability to make a profit.

Entrepreneurs often buy into the old motivational cliché, "Believe it and you can achieve it." That is just flat-out wrong. I believe I can be successful; therefore, I can achieve success. No, that's not how it works. Besides it doesn't matter whether you believe in what you are doing nearly as much as it matters whether the marketplace believes in what you are doing. You can believe you are adding value but if customers don't believe it, then what you believe is a waste of energy.

There are as many opportunities to be successful in business as there are people who are successful in business. There are a million ways to make a living. But don't believe you can be successful choosing a business just because someone else is doing well at it. Don't believe your success can duplicate another's. We all bring something unique to the marketplace; figure out what yours is before you try to duplicate what someone else has done.

Some tough questions

What is your skill-set? What do you have the ability to do—and do really well—to the point that the market will choose you and not someone already doing it? What uniqueness do you bring to an already crowded market? Do you have the experience to sell? Do you understand messaging and marketing? Do you know the difference between selling and marketing? Do you know how to hire and fire? Do you know how to manage people? Do you know how to create a business plan? Do you know how to manage systems and processes? Do you know how to read a balance sheet? Are you absolutely clear about the problem that exists that you have an answer for? Do you know what the problem is costing people? Have you identified and quantified the pain and the problem so your solution is a better, more justifiable expense than living with the pain? Do you know how to deliver great customer service? Do you know how to negotiate when buying as well as when selling? Have you studied other successful entrepreneurs? Do you have a written-down plan to ensure success? Do you have a written-down plan for what to do when things go wrong? Do you have a trusted list of mentors or coaches to help you when you need it?

That's a big list of questions, I know. But not being able to answer them correctly means that you either have a lot more preparation to do before you go into business or you need to keep your day job because you aren't ready and will likely fail.

Workspace Decisions

Where are you going to work? These days, if you've got a laptop that's all you need, right? Maybe. Possibly. Probably not. A laptop is just one thing you need. For some businesses, a dedicated brick and mortar location is required. For many solopreneurs, a corner of the bedroom might work.

My suggestion is to let the money make the decision for you. If you don't have the money to rent space, then don't rent space. When starting out, choose the option you can afford. Too many businesses build out beautiful offices or the perfect retail space or other business space and then their money is gone and they can't afford the upkeep because their revenue doesn't justify it.

If you are a solopreneur trying to work from home, I would suggest your workspace have a door. If you're trying to work from home in an open area or in a corner of a room and you don't have a way to shut off the rest of the world, you're going to be in trouble. Distractions can cost you money. And everything can be a distraction—from the kids, the cat sitting on your laptop or the dog snoring too loudly. I have experience with that last one. Leon, my bulldog, can snore so loudly I can't get my work done. But regardless of the distraction, it can give you an excuse to do something other than do what is profitable. If you are looking for a reason not to do the hard stuff and get the work done, then a snoring dog is just as good of an excuse as any other. When I don't want to work, and I have had plenty of times in my life when I didn't really want to do the work, then I can totally embrace the slightest of distractions.

I avoid those excuses for not doing the work by avoiding the distractions. That means controlling the environment. I have a door that closes and locks. When I close that door to work, I dedicate myself to working. I don't eat or do personal things at my desk. In fact, I don't do anything at my desk except work. It goes back to what I've said earlier about discipline: I have the discipline to say, when I'm at my desk I will do desk work. If I'm tired of doing the desk work or when the work is finished, then I will get up and leave my desk, and go to another place where I don't do work. I have created this workspace in my home and enforce it with discipline.

If you are in a place where you can't avoid the distractions that come from being at home, and if you can afford it, then I have no problem with you renting office space or one of the coworking spaces that have become popular. However if you go to a coworking space, you're throwing yourself back in a situation of having people around that you can socialize with as well as many other ways to kill time. Focus, focus, focus. You've got to focus on adding dollars to your bottom line.

Solopreneurs sometimes complain about loneliness. Working alone in that home office day after day, without having people around you, can at times feel lonely. The pandemic proved to many just how lonely it can be to be stuck in your home without the ability to get out. This was not an issue for me. I like being alone and am not lonely when I am by myself. Many years ago I heard Wayne Dyer, one of the personal development greats, say "The only time you're lonely is when you don't like the person you are alone with." I like me. I don't require a lot of heavy socialization or interaction. Here's my motivational idea for you to deal with the loneliness of being a solopreneur: Like yourself. Yep, that's a great place to start. If you are full of self-doubt, this business won't work for you. If you need the constant ego-boost that comes from surrounding yourself with sycophants, forget it. If you need coworkers and teammates and people in your life all the time, keep your day job. Just like the business is all up to you, YOU are all up to you as well. You need to approve of you. That confidence comes from you being clear about what you are doing and why you are doing it, and by having a good idea about what you are doing—at least most of the time. Confidence comes from clarity. That's why this book is written to create the doubt and to ask the tough questions about your readiness. It's better that I ask the tough questions of you here before you start, than your getting blind-sided by the problems of starting your own business after you have taken the plunge and risked it all.

I have a lot of experience with being alone. Over the past thirty years, I have spent as many as 200 to 250 days a year on the road. When you are by yourself on an airplane, driving to the airport, in your rental car, or in your hotel, and the only time you see other people is when you are looking at them from the stage or when you are at the back of the room signing books, you realize just how lonely the business can be. I grew to enjoy it as I worked hard on being someone I enjoy. That's why it is so important for you to like you. And while that's not what this book is about, it is an important factor in your success as an entrepreneur. Plus, I've written many bestselling books that can help you with that idea as well.

Social media

More than half of the world's population is on social media. On average, we are on social media well over two hours per day, and that number is on the rise with each passing day. Your business cannot exist without a social media presence. You pretty much have to have Facebook, YouTube, Instagram, Clubhouse and the myriad of other social media platforms to engage your customer base and build a following as well as communicate your value to potential customers. And by the time you read this book, many more social media platforms will have come, and many will have gone.

However, social media has become anything but social. It's become mean and vitriolic and a place for the keyboard cowards to attack you, your business, your thoughts, ideas, and opinions. Be careful playing with the trolls on social media. The more you argue and defend, the more vulnerable you become to them. You just can't make yourself susceptible to that sort of thing if you are running a business.

If you are relying on social media for your social contact, just understand that it is no longer very sociable. You probably already know this but as an entrepreneur it's good to be reminded.

Social media has a very necessary place in running your business. But as far as your life is concerned, you need more social interaction than what takes place only on a screen. Figure out ways to enjoy your life outside of sitting at the desk. Involve yourself in community affairs. Involve yourself more with your family. Get a handful of friends you can talk to. Early in my career, one of the best things I ever did was to surround myself with a handful of trusted friends with whom I can truly be Larry Winget, with no agenda and no pretense. If you've got a handful of friends like that consider yourself fortunate.

I suggest that you keep your business social media separate from your personal social media. I have a business presence where the public is welcome to interact with me on what I post. I do my best to keep that page only about what I do for a living. I wasn't always that disciplined. However, when someone said that my dog was ugly, that crossed the line for me.

A few years ago, I painstakingly went through all the contacts on my personal pages and deleted anyone who wasn't a "real" friend. I went from the limit of five thousand friends on my personal Facebook page to just a few hundred. That decision was one of my best. On my personal page, with true friends, I post pictures of my family and my personal life. I don't add anyone to that list unless they are someone I know well, or have known well, and with whom I share some significant history.

On my business page, I am careful to stay away from politics and other subjects. My business pages are just that: business. Those are the pages where I share business advice, ideas and opinions about business and where I promote what I do for a living. Too many entrepreneurs blur the lines between their personal and business pages to the point it costs them friends as well as business. Keep them separate.

Do what you uniquely can do

Many years ago, I heard Robert Schuller, founder of the Crystal Cathedral as well as bestselling inspirational author, say, "I do what I uniquely can do and hire others to do what they uniquely can do. Only I can give the sermons and write the books. For everything else, I hire someone else to do it." Those were true words of inspiration as well as great advice for me at the time. In my business, only I can give the speeches. Only I can do the recordings and shoot the videos and do the television appearances. Only I can write the books. Someone else can easily do everything else.

At the beginning, you probably can't afford to hire someone else and you are going to be the chief cook and bottle washer. You are going to be the CEO and the janitor. That's fine. It's a humbling experience and teaches you the value of all that has to be done to keep your business afloat. However, there will come a time when you move past that and will need to look for help.

When your business has grown to the point where you can afford to hire people to do the things that can easily be off-loaded from you, then hire them to do it. Then you can do more of what only you uniquely can do. There is somebody out there in the world who is willing to do just about anything you can dream up that you need to have done. I'm certainly a believer in delegating or hiring what can be done when you can afford to. We hear this a lot: "I'm a big picture person. I'm not much into details." Well, either you learn how to get really good at the details or you hire somebody who can do that for you. You always hire to your weakness.

Every solopreneur needs to figure out what they uniquely can do, not because you think no one else can do it, but because literally no one else can do it. But keep your ego in check here. You're probably not as big a deal as you think you are. You can do more of what you want to convince yourself you need to offload. Hiring someone to do what you don't like to do is not what I'm talking about here. While someone else could easily do a good portion of what you do, that doesn't mean you overextend yourself by creating a payroll and tax liability just because you are lazy. Do the work all by yourself for as long as you possibly can.

So, to recap, do what you can uniquely can do and when it comes time to hire someone, hire someone who will leave you doing what you uniquely can do to make the business the most amount of profit.

Hire someone to do the rest when you can afford it and when you hire, hire true professionals and pay them what they are worth. We've all bought cheap and been sorry for it down the road. And every business owner has hired cheap and then paid to have the job done over again. Don't be one of those people. Spend enough money to get a true professional. I saw a great quote in Seth Godin's book, *This Is Marketing*. He said that the Internet is full of websites created by amateurs who really like what they've done. But they should have hired a professional so others would really like it.

That's the case with a lot of solopreneurs. They're out there creating a business, a product, content, a website, and possibly books or audio/video or training programs. They are creating what they like only to find out that nobody else likes it. They find out too late that their potential customers don't like it. If you aren't a website designer, don't create your own website. I've seen landscapers do their own website before. They should have stuck to landscaping because their website is costing them business, not getting them business. Stick with what you do best!

Structuring Your Time

Solopreneurs often struggle with structuring their time. This is another area where people have to play to their strengths and hire to their weaknesses. One of my strengths is that I know the time of day when I am at my best. When you know that, you can put the most important things into those time frames for maximum achievement. For instance, I know that early in the morning is just not my best time. I'm not a morning person, I've never been a morning person and I am never going to be a morning person. I don't get up early to do anything unless I am being paid to do it. I hate the whole idea of 7:00 a.m. Some people are great first thing in the morning. I'm great around nine or ten o'clock. I am at my very best between ten and two o'clock. Those are my optimum working hours, which means that is when I'm going to do everything that's most important. In my case, I do most of my podcasts, interviews, and writing when my brain is at the highest level of functioning. Outside of those hours, I have some flexibility, because many things still have to be done that don't require maximum brain capacity. I can do them when I'm not at my very best. And I don't let the mundane things that have to be done in every business interrupt my prime time. Yes, it does require some structuring.

Figure out when you're at your very best, but don't be stupid about it. Don't say, "I'm just not a morning person, so I'm not going to start until noon." That's dumb. I often work outside of my "best time." I give speeches and do interviews and coaching calls way before 9:00 a.m. I have done television at 3:00 a.m. It was harder for me, but I did it because that's what the job required. You do what the job requires because it's your JOB! Being able to do your job when you are at your best is typically a luxury you can't afford early on so don't use that as an excuse.

Here's another hint for you solopreneurs who work from home: Never work in your pajamas. Get up and put on your clothes. Dress for work just like you did in the days of having a job. When I used to do a lot of radio interviews and podcasts, I would put on the full Larry Winget package—the cowboy shirts, the cowboy boots, the starched jeans—because I knew that I performed better when I was stage ready, just like I was going to walk out onstage. For me, that meant putting on the right attire to help me get there mentally. I don't have to do that anymore—because I've been doing this for thirty years—but putting on work clothes puts you in the right frame of mind to do work. Pajamas and a robe are for night-time, not work-time.

I liked the old days when people dressed up for work, because I believe people work better when they're dressed properly for it. I was never a fan of casual Friday that evolved into casual every single day. I know there are jobs where it doesn't matter. It might not matter on the outside and your customers might not ever see you. And it might not matter to your boss. However, I believe it matters to who you are on the inside. Looking your best changes the way you feel about yourself. Just as making your bed is important because the bed is the biggest thing in the bedroom and when the bed is made, everything about the bedroom looks better. Make your bed and make yourself.

When you get up in the morning, shower, shave or put on your makeup, brush your teeth and comb your hair—whatever is appropriate for you. Clean yourself up and get ready to go to work. Put on the right attire, as if you're going to work, and then go to work. I don't care if going to work means walking to the corner of the bedroom to your desk, do it. I promise you, it's more than just a trick. You will do better work when you're dressed for work. It's a discipline that yields tangible results.

Bottom line

To conclude this chapter, I want to repeat that the number one thing required for long-term business success is

6

Building a
Superstar Staff

The two biggest problems in business

Easily, the two biggest problems in business today are employees and customers. If all of us could just figure out how to run a business with no employees, think of the headaches we could all avoid.

Imagine how smoothly your business would run if you didn't have anyone to supervise, or to manage, or to train. Wouldn't it be great if you didn't have to fix their mistakes or navigate their emotions? And think how much money you would have if you didn't have to pay them! What if you didn't have customers to make happy or to handle their complaints. I can only imagine! Of course, you wouldn't have any money, but still it's something to think about, right?

But the reality is, you have to have customers and everything that goes with that. And at some point, you will have employees even it's only a subcontractor.

I have talked a lot so far about the importance of the customer, as they are responsible for the revenue that comes to your business. Now, it's time to talk about employees.

Even as a solopreneur, you will have employees. If not in the true sense of the word, then in the sense that you will subcontract projects for a period of time to accomplish something you don't have the time or expertise to handle.

You are always going to rely on others at some level and that will require managing those people, coaching them, communicating with them, training them and leading them. No one succeeds completely all on their own.

Taking Care of Customers

If most people were asked to evaluate business in America today, I bet they would say that business, on the whole, is a mess. I would agree with them. Businesses have gotten really good at selling their goods and services by hook or by crook. For the most part, they will do and say whatever it takes to get the money out of the customers pockets and into their own. Many have confused selling with spamming. They constantly fill your social media and inbox and mailbox with your need for what they have with no research, and without a care whether you need it or want it. They know that wearing you down will eventually work. And while this is not the case for most businesses, enough make use of these practices that it has made people skeptical of the integrity of those in business. As a result, too many people think that businesses have gotten really good at taking care of themselves, but not so good at taking care of their customers.

If the average person were to evaluate their customer experience from start to finish with most of the businesses they have dealt with in the past year, they would not give those businesses very high marks. Why is that? Probably because they felt hustled, or overpromised and underserved, or they didn't feel appreciated or important or respected.

When this happens, and it happens every day, it's because the business has forgotten how their business works. Your number one priority in business is to make money: I've been really clear about that. You make money by getting it out of the hands of the customers and into your pockets. The way you do that is by serving them well and solving their problems. This simple process hinges on "serving them well and solving their problems."

Most businesses aren't focused nearly enough on solving customers' problems as they are on getting their money. Yet problem-solving is the key to making the money. The more problems you solve, and the higher the costs of those problems, the more money you will make.

When you start your business, you have to have complete clarity on the problem you solve. Then you have to be clear about the pain that the problem causes in the lives or businesses of others. Most eventually figure this out but aren't great at communicating that message when hiring employees and growing their company. They focus on hiring to get tasks done and the message about solving problems and alleviating pain gets lost.

You must communicate to your employees what they have been hired to do not only in terms of the tasks they must accomplish but to illustrate to them that those tasks lead to solving the customer's problem. Each employee has to comprehend their role in why the company exists, not only in terms of profitability, but in understanding that problems are being solved.

Too many owners and managers hire people the wrong way—by communicating only what is being sold or providing only a list of things they must do each day. Employees must understand their role in the bigger picture. When they do, they appreciate why it is important to complete their tasks and see that their contribution matters.

The Generational Gap

One of the biggest challenges in business today is the generational gap between boomers, millennials, Gen X, and Gen Z.

Boomers, for the most part, took a job and went to work so they could buy stuff. I know that was the case for me. I didn't have much stuff. I wanted stuff. It took money to buy stuff. I went to work to make money so I could buy stuff. Very basic and simple, linear thinking. The job didn't matter, the stuff mattered.

Millennials typically think differently on this subject. Studies say that money is not first on their list of priorities. Instead, they want to feel they are part of something that makes a difference. If you are hiring or managing millennials, help them feel they are part of something by explaining to them the problem your company solves and the pain that it alleviates.

Ask them how they see themselves making a contribution and they will have more buy-in to why your company is in business. Most employees in any generation aren't opposed to your business making a profit when they see that others benefit.

All employees want to feel they are contributing to something bigger than sweeping the floor, running the cash register, or making the sales calls. The task itself is secondary to the mission of the job. Every job has a mission, and that mission is to serve the customer well, to help the customer overcome their problem, and to stop feeling the pain caused by the problem.

This is not only important when hiring people but also to impress on the people who are already on your payroll. When every single person on the payroll understands the role they play in solving customer problems, your business will be more successful, you'll have more camaraderie among workers, and your customers will start to feel the care and respect that emanates from people who are there to help them.

Hire Slow, Fire Fast

One of my chief maxims about employees is to hire slow and fire fast. Anyone who has ever had employees has made the mistake of doing just the opposite. We hire fast, sometimes out of desperation, and realize pretty quickly we are stuck with a bad hire. We don't take the time to vet the employee.

You've got to take your time to find the right fit for the opening you're trying to fill. First ask yourself if you can get by without hiring someone. If you can, then do that. Save the money. It's expensive to hire and train and more expensive to terminate. But if you have to fill the vacancy, then figure out exactly what the job really requires. And I mean more than tasks. What type of personality best fits the job? Does it require somebody who's good at interacting with others? Then hire somebody who's good at interacting with others. Most people hire for skill set. That's fine but that's only a small part of any job. I love it when people have the skill set as it's a time saver, for sure. But I would never hire skill set first. I would hire for personality and values. Will that individual's personality fit the overall personality and image of our organization? Do they have the right values? Honesty, integrity, appreciation, respect. While those values are hard skills to interview for, you can tell a lot about a person with a good conversation. That means you don't hire just based on a written resume. If the job requires talking to other people—from coworkers to customers—then you need to talk to that person. Ask them what they think about the values of honesty, integrity, doing the right thing, showing appreciation, and respect of others. When you interview someone who shows up on time, is presentable, can look you in the eye, says please and thank you, and shows you respect, that's probably a clue as to how they're going to treat other people.

We all have the ability to notice these things, but we get in a hurry when hiring and get more concerned with the work that needs to be done rather than the person we are hiring to do that work.

Can they operate this piece of machinery? Can they run a cash register? Have they worked for a competitor? Good. Then they know what to do and how to do it. But that doesn't mean they are a good person of good values. They have tactical skills, but they still might be a bad person. Hire good people above all. Everything else can be trained.

Fire fast. Is it possible to fire fast? What's the right way to do it? Go back to what I said earlier in this book about making sure you are legal in all you do. This is becoming more of an issue than ever before. More regulations pop up at a state and federal level seemingly every day and it's impossible to stay current unless that is your job, and as a typical business owner it isn't.

Therefore, I am not going to talk about legalities as I am not a lawyer and because every state is different. What you can do based on your right to work laws and so forth is going to be different based on your own state's laws. Just be aware we have become a litigious society, where anybody can and probably will sue anybody else for anything, at any time.

However, here are some general rules to make this easier for you. First of all, always document everything. Typically, in an argument over employment, the one with the most paper wins. Make sure you can say this matter was discussed on this date and at this time and the employee signed off that it happened. Documentation, daily if necessary, per occurrence if necessary, to make sure that you have absolutely perfect records when it comes to what you expect, what was discussed, and what was communicated, and proof that you have the employee's agreement in writing that it happened can be of great value. Yes, it's a pain, but go through the pain as it will be worth it.

Then, when the employee doesn't perform properly according to the agreed instructions, you've pretty much got the laws on your side. Maybe. Possibly. Probably. The problem is that people don't document well. These days, you can't afford to be sloppy in hiring, and certainly not in firing, and not in documentation.

Even in the face of the litigious society we live in right now, I still believe in getting rid of bad employees as quickly as possible. In my experience, in the long run, it's cheaper to fight somebody when they are on the outside of your company than when they are on the inside. A bad employee who still works for you can hurt you with your customers, undermine you with other employees and destroy your credibility as a leader. It can be a real mess in more ways than you can imagine.

Not long ago, I coached a small company for a year. Every call I had with them mentioned a salesman I'll call Bob. He was a problem for every person in the company. It was always "Bob did this, and Bob did that." But they also said, "Bob's been around a long time, and Bob's our number one salesperson in terms of revenue."

From the first time I talked to them, I said, "Fire Bob. Fire Bob today." I told them to just hand the phone to Bob right now and I will fire Bob for you! I explained how Bob was ruining their company. I told them that their employees considered the tolerance of Bob's bad behavior as acceptable and as a result, their own behavior was becoming more like Bob's. I explained that they lost credibility as leaders every day they put up with good ol' Bob.

It took months and months to get the company to take action because they valued his sales more than they valued their other employees or even their customers. And I know it's hard to fire your number one revenue producer, regardless of how toxic they are. However, they did finally fire him. The entire performance of the rest of the sales team improved. Customer complaints went way down. Morale within the company improved. Respect of management improved. It turns out that the old cliché of "One bad apple spoils the whole barrel" is absolutely true. Get rid of the bad apple fast. Yes, Bob filed a complaint once he was fired, but it was still cheaper for the company in the long run to pay to fight him on the outside of the company than it was to deal with what he was costing them from the inside.

Training is expensive but worth it

The cost of an untrained workforce is greater than the cost of the training. Yet training is an area that typically is the first to get cut when the economy is tough, or a business is struggling. And that's a bad idea. And any time you start thinking that the cost of education is expensive, try the cost of ignorance.

It truly is a shame that the first thing I see cut when times get hard is the training budget. That's exactly the opposite of what should be done. If I were having financial trouble, I would spend more money on sales training immediately. I would hire a professional sales trainer to come in and work with my sales force to make sure that they were able to increase the volume of sales as well as the size of the ticket they were selling. I would do whatever it took to increase the revenue coming in, and selling is the fastest way to do that.

Here's the problem with training budgets and how we train people ourselves: typically, we train people on how to do their jobs. The truth is that most people do their jobs pretty well. I'm convinced of that. We're not suffering from bad service because people don't know how to do their jobs. We suffer from bad service because people don't care if they do their jobs well or not. And people who don't care if they do their jobs well are not good people. They don't have good core values.

If you are going to train your people, you should train them how to be better people. When I ran my tele-communications company many years ago, I had fifty people working for me. I spent money training them with Zig Ziglar's course on being better people, setting and achieving goals, treating people well, and communicating better. None of that training had anything to do with selling or installing telephone systems. My employees all knew how to sell and install telephone systems. However, they weren't good at setting goals, communicating well with each other, or showing respect for each other. My goal was to get us to go back to the basic values of what it took to be good people.

When you improve somebody's ability to set goals, their sales numbers go up. When you teach people how to be better people, every aspect of their job improves. Spend money teaching your people how to be better people and it will reap dividends far beyond what you ever imagined.

The struggle for many business owners is changing your mind about what's really important. How to do the job is important, but again I contend most people know how to do their jobs. Yes, they could do their jobs better. And they could do their jobs faster. But when you teach people how to show respect and appreciation, how to communicate better, how to set goals and achieve them, you make that person a better human being. Good people typically do good work. Not every time for sure, but certainly most of the time.

I have always said that you can't get a good deal from a bad guy. You can for a while but not long term because sooner or later, who they are drives what they do. I spent a lot of years trying to get good work out of people who weren't good people. I did get it, but not for long. Finally after much frustration, I decided it would be a huge savings of my time, energy, and money just to hire good people and teach them how to do good work instead of hiring good workers and teaching them how to be good people.

We need to focus on teaching people the right values and we need to reward those values. People will make mistakes. That's okay, I've made lots of mistakes. People will mess up. They'll be sorry; they'll wish they had done it differently. But if you've trained them, worked with them, and honored them for their honesty, integrity, hard work, appreciation, respect, and all those other values, you'll end up with a smarter, better workforce that creates better results, and you'll have a much happier customer base as a result.

In short, hire primarily for values, character qualities, and work ethic. Do that knowing that you can train that type of person to do just about anything in terms of tasks.

I've written six *New York Times/Wall Street Journal* bestsellers teaching people how to do any number of things. I've written books about how to handle your finances, how to be a better parent, how to run a better business, how to be a better person and how to achieve more. All of the books are full of how-to tactics and strategies. I'm giving you lots of how-to tactics in this book as well. Sadly, here is what I have discovered: you can give people all of the tools on how to do things better and they will indeed do better—but not for long. People always go back to who they are inside and not what they know they need to do or are being paid to do on the outside. If your employee is a bad person and you give them a list of good things to do, they will do it—but not for long, because they are not good people.

I figured out that what was wrong with my approach for all of those years was that I was trying to give bad people good things to do. That's why now I focus more on core values and helping people become better from the inside out. Good people will eventually figure out the right things to do. It may not be pretty, it may not be perfect, it may not be the way you wanted, but they will do the right thing because they are good people. If you refocus your efforts toward helping your employees learn what it takes to become better human beings, then they will eventually do enough right things and you will see more success from their efforts.

Hire the right people and help them become even better as human beings as well as training them in the skills that they need for their jobs. It's that combination that works. We cannot teach the skills and ignore the human. We've got to focus on the human being, and then teach them the skills.

Teamwork Doesn't Work

Today we hear a lot about the glories of teamwork. My position is pretty much the opposite: Teamwork doesn't work. Why? Because someone on that team isn't going to work. Let's use a sports team as an example. The team really performs well, and they get a trophy. Everybody steps forward to get their trophy. One guy steps forward, and everybody on that team is looking at him knowing full-well he didn't do a damn thing. They know. He knows as well. Yet, he happily steps up and accepts the glory that he didn't contribute to.

It's the same in business: someone on your business team isn't going to work. They aren't contributing. Everyone knows it. But every time something is achieved, they stake their claim on the success. Success is not achieved by the collective effort of a team. Success is achieved by a group of superstar individuals who share a common goal. Even though the superstars may not get along with each other, they respect one another and their contributions and they get the job done. There is certainly a long history of teammates not getting along with each other but respecting each other's skills and talents to the point where they work well toward the common goal of winning the game.

You can have your team and I will take the group of superstars who get it done because they are individuals who excel by themselves as well as know how to work together. Teamwork doesn't work because there is always someone who won't work. Individuals who are superstars always work. I'll take them every single time.

By the way, if there's anything that bothers me among the teamwork promoters out there it's when I hear one of them say, "It doesn't matter who gets the credit." Bull. I want the credit every time I do something well. If I did the work, then of course I want the credit. Don't you? Can you imagine not caring who gets the credit for a job well done? "It doesn't matter. You don't have to pat me on the back. We all did this together." No, there's a better than good chance that we didn't all do it together. Some-one did it and they deserve the acknowledgment. And when you do recognize their excellence, they will work even harder to do well again and again and again.

I don't understand people who don't care who gets the credit. I want people who fight hard and work their butts off to make sure the job was done well just so they can get the credit.

There was a time when I worked as a salesperson for the telephone company. There were people who were only 85 percent of quota who made more money than I did, because they had more time with the company than I did. They've been there ten years but they were 85 percent of quota and I was 300 percent of quota? That's why I am no fan of tenure and am more of a fan of performance.

The whole concept of this wonderful group of people who go in and get it all done with no one needing to take any special credit is crazy to me. Give me the superstar employees who want the credit and will work their butts off to get it.

People love to say that there is no *I* in *team*. It's become a motivational cliché. There is no *I* in team, but there is an *M* and there is an *E*, and I'm taking care of me. That's the kind of employee I want to hire: one who makes sure the work gets done, regardless of what someone else does.

You might say, "Larry, if I bring this group of superstar individuals together and people care who gets the credit, and they're competing with one another internally, won't that create a more toxic corporate culture?"

I have to laugh at that idea. I like competition and people perform better when there is competition. I recently read a study about how people actually enjoy competition in the workplace, and we are doing our best to rob them of it. We are competitive at our very core. It's who we are. It's the reason our species exists to this day. It is survival of the fittest. The smartest, the hardest working, the best achievers who bring excellence to all they do will always survive.

I like a little healthy, respectful competition. I don't think that creates toxicity in the workplace. I do think it can be great fun if managed correctly. If competition becomes toxic, that has to be thrown squarely in the lap of the leader. Toxicity is the responsibility of the leader to control.

When someone complains about someone else doing well instead of improving their own performance, that might be a person you don't want to have working for you. I don't want somebody who complains about how well a coworker is doing based on their own hard work and achievement. I want somebody who sees the excellence in others as a challenge to doing better himself and steps up accordingly.

We spend way too much time handing out participation trophies in business, just as we do in kindergarten. Business is not about participation, it's about performance. Businesses who don't perform, soon won't be participating in the marketplace.

Motivating Salespeople

Motivators are just a means to move people from where they are to a different place. One thing that motivates salespeople is money. And if money doesn't motivate your salespeople, that might be a clue that you've hired the wrong salespeople. That's why I like compensation plans that are based on performance. I like commissioned sales programs. It gives salespeople the incentive to make the calls and close the sales. And it proves to them that when they get the quality of their sales effort and the quantity of their sales efforts working for them, they will get paid well for it. That's a great motivator.

No one is special

One of the most controversial things I've ever written was in my parenting book, *Your Kids Are Your Own Fault*. I wrote that your kids aren't special. That fired up a lot of parents. I said that your kids are special to you because you gave them life and they are yours. However, in the real world, their value will be based on their contribution. It will be about how much work they get done and how well they do that work. Their contribution to the marketplace and to society will determine what the marketplace and society think of them. They're special to you by birth; the rest of the world will judge them by what they contribute.

That idea fired a lot of people up, because they want every human being, every employee, to be special.

The truth is that in business, we are all measured by the contribution we make to the bottom line of the business who pays us. In the workplace, the person who contributes the most gets the most recognition. The person who's just filling the hole, who's barely breathing, doesn't deserve the same recognition or financial reward as the superstar employee.

That's just the way business works. If you are not worth more than you cost, then you are a liability and must be eliminated to bring in someone who adds value instead of subtracting it. If you are not a source of revenue, then you are a liability. Liabilities must be removed as they are too expensive to employ.

Culture

Business owners are concerned about creating the right corporate culture. They should be concerned. I think it's funny when entrepreneurs tell me they have hired someone to help them create a culture. They fail to realize their company already has a culture. You can hire someone to help you fix your culture but never think you don't have one already. A culture is just the way you do things habitually. If you do the same thing over and over to the point that your entire company does it that way, that has become your corporate culture. It is the habitual repetition of actions and beliefs that creates your culture. You already have a corporate culture.

Your culture, the way you do things, is always based on what you believe to be most important. You don't have to tell me what it is, it shows in how you sell, serve and manage. It is based on your core values.

Your business practices reflect your culture, and your culture is the result of your values. If your practices are messed up, your sales will be low, your customers will be unhappy, you'll have a toxic work environment, and you will have coworkers at each other's throats. As a result of your practices, your culture is messed up and your results will be messed up. It's that simple. Bad results are the result of bad actions and bad actions are the result of bad values.

If you have honest people with integrity, who show appreciation, who treat others with respect, your culture will automatically reflect that. So will your processes, your actions, and your results. Many nuances come into play here and there are many factors at work, but this is the bottom line.

Larry's Dirty Dozen

I am going to conclude this chapter with a set of ideas that I call Larry's Dirty Dozen Employer Handbook. I have been sharing these ideas for years with companies of all sizes from every industry. They are an especially good guide for new entrepreneurs who are looking to establish ground rules for employees.

1. You must set high expectations for every single employee. At that point, you have to clearly communicate those expectations and manage according to them. Once you've set the expectations, communicated them, and managed toward them, you've got to inspect what you expect.

2. Be decisive. Of course, it's important to make the right decision, but there comes a time when you just need to make the decision, then make your decision right. Odds are that you're not going to be right all the time; even so, you have been decisive.

3. Don't concern yourself with being liked; instead, spend your energy doing whatever it takes to be respected. It's great if your employees like you but it is critical that they respect you.

4. Pay people well. You can't expect to get rich when you're keeping somebody else broke. And never forget that you should never mess with people's money.

You told them what they would be paid and when you would pay them. You made a deal. Honor that deal and if you can't afford to keep the deal, then cut them loose so they can go elsewhere.

5. Disrespect is immediate grounds for dismissal. Without exception. If someone disrespects their boss, the company they work for, their coworkers, the customer, even the competition, they should be fired. Respectful discussion and disagreement are allowed, but disrespect will not be tolerated.

6. Discover your uniqueness as a business and as an employer. This will allow you to compete better in the marketplace as well as attract better employees.

7. If it's broken, fix it now. Most people recognize that something is broken and wait too long to give it the proper attention. Whatever it is continues to deteriorate, and the little problem becomes a little bit bigger problem. Then the little bit bigger problem becomes a pretty significant problem. When ignored, that significant problem can become a huge problem and ultimately cause your failure. So when you see a little problem, fix it immediately. Don't wait. Nip it in the bud.

8. Reward life skills and personal growth among your employees. Spend your time, energy, and money helping people become better people.

9. A deal is a deal. Keep your word. I don't care how inconvenient or embarrassing it might be for you. I don't care if it costs you money. If you said it, you do it.

10. Fire people when they need to be fired. What you tolerate, you endorse. What you put up with, you support. If you let people continue their bad behavior then you are supporting and endorsing that behavior.

11. When hiring, be aware of "articulate incompetents." These are people who talk a good game but can't deliver it. They have all the right language to make you feel good about them. Then you hire them and they can't do the job.

12. The last one is just this: Keep it simple. If it feels really complicated, you need to stop, evaluate, simplify, and begin again. Success in business is just not that hard. It comes down to solving people's problems, alleviating their pain, showing them how you are able to do that, gaining their trust by caring about

what they're going through, and then selling them your value with great service to back it all up. Show genuine appreciation for the money they've shared with you and the trust they have placed in you. You do that and you will be successful in business.

7

Serve Customers the Way They Want to Be Served

If you were to ask businesspeople what they think is most essential to business success, they would probably say profitability. It's technically true as far as it goes, but in reality they are focusing on an effect, not a cause. The main cause of profitability is serving customers, and serving them far better than your competition.

In fact, customer service will be what sets you apart from the competition. Chances are that people can buy your products and services from any number of different companies. They can even get it cheaper somewhere else. But service is the differentiator. If customers love your product and your price, yet your service is questionable, they will stop doing business with you and will pay more to do business with someone else who serves them better.

Bad Service Has A Big Mouth

Most of the service that we receive as customers is pretty good. We really don't pay much attention to good customer service unless it is truly outstanding. However, we always remember bad service and are quick to tell others about it.

The idea of serving people well seems to have slipped to the wayside. Many businesses act as if they're entitled to their customers' money—until they hit a downturn. Then out of desperation, they'll do anything to promise their customers great service.

All of those companies that never paid any attention to me after I bought from them were suddenly very interested in me during the pandemic. They hadn't said a word to me in years, yet now, they want to act like they are my best friend and I am their best customer. Why? Because when business was good and they had more business than they could handle, they didn't have to provide me with great appreciation and follow-up. They sold me and moved on to the next customer. I became a distant memory quickly. But when the pandemic hit, I started getting emails and phone calls saying, "Larry, just checking in to see how you're doing."

I haven't heard a word in years and suddenly they are doing welfare checks on me. I know you got those same kinds of calls. I was always quick to reply with something like, "You don't really care how I'm doing. The fact is, your business is not doing well and you're scrambling to make money. You're calling me to kiss up to me to excuse the fact that I haven't heard from you in three years, and you're asking if there's a way I'll spend some more money with you."

You're probably not as direct as I am, but you should be. We need to call companies on that sort of stuff. We need to remind them that they've got to take care of us during good times so they don't have to beg for our business during bad times.

Service is not something you do every once in a while; it is something you do all the time.

Good Service is Rooted In Respect

I was recently remodeling an area of my house. I'd been working with an electrician for years and I really liked him. He is a good guy and his prices are great. He does good work, and he cleans up after himself. He just has one problem: he can't seem to show up when he says he will. We will agree to a day and a time and without a doubt, he will show up two hours late. He knows this bothers me. I have made it perfectly clear to him. I finally started saying, "Call me when you are headed in my direction. Just call and let me know, so I know you're twenty minutes out."

One day, after I had let the electrician pick the date and time to do the work, I said to him, "You call and let me know when you are on your way to my house."

"I'll be there by 8:30," he said.

"No, you won't," I said. "You're never here by 8:30. You always tell me that. You just call me when you're on the way."

He called me at 8:15 and said, "I'm about twenty minutes out."

"That sounds great, can't wait to see you," I said.

He showed up at 10:45. I said, "I don't know where you were leaving from when you called me at 8:15, but I'm having a hard time believing it was two and a half hours away."

"I had to make a couple of stops along the way."

"Then why did you call me and say you were on the way?"

"Why are you busting my chops, Larry? Why are you so upset?"

"I've been doing business with you for a number of years. I like your work. I've referred you to people, but I'll never refer you to anybody else again. In fact, I'm never even going to use you again, because you show so little respect for me. Your work is good, I like it, but I would rather pay more money to somebody I don't know and have them show up when they tell me they're going to show up. My money isn't worth as much to me as my time, and you disrespect my time."

"I don't even understand what you're talking about," he said.

"You're right, you don't, and because you don't understand, we're not going to be able to do business together again." I stopped using him. He didn't even get to finish that day's work. His lack of respect for me and my time cost him all of my business, and I used him a lot. It cost him all of the referral business I had given him over the years. His work and prices didn't lose him all of that money, his lack of respect cost him that money.

I did this electrician a favor by telling him in detail why he lost my business. Most customers won't go to the trouble of expressing their dissatisfaction with bad service. I believe when you don't express your dissatisfaction in detail for the experience you've been through that you become an accessory to the crime for the bad service the next person is about to receive. You have actually helped this business deliver bad service by not pointing out to them what they did wrong and how they could have done better.

Remember that what you put up with, you condone. Do you condone bad service? If not, then why do you put up with it? Do you condone rudeness? Then why do you put up with it? Do you condone stealing? Why do you let your employees sit around and do personal work on their computer? That's stealing. Why do you put up with that? If you don't bring it to their attention, if you don't stop tolerating their bad behavior and putting up with bad service, rudeness, lateness, etc., then you are putting your stamp of approval on it. That ought to make you reconsider how you deal with bad service in the future and start thinking about how customers should be dealing with the bad service you or your employees give them. The best thing a customer can do for you is what I did for my electrician: explain to you what you did wrong so you can fix it with the next customer.

When somebody explains what you have done wrong and you respond with, "Thank you; I appreciate that and I'm sorry. What can I do to make it right? I can assure you it won't happen in the future," then it's likely that they will forgive you. Most people are willing to forgive when someone takes responsibility and offers a sincere apology.

An electrician like mine, who said, "I don't even understand; why are you busting my chops for this?" was never going to learn. All he had to do was say, "I'm sorry. You're right and I guarantee that it won't happen again," and I would have given him another chance. He lost money, he lost reputation, he lost future work, and he lost referrals—all because of a small show of disrespect. While it was no big deal in his mind, it was a huge show of disrespect in my mind.

Treat the customer how the customer wants to be treated, not how you believe it's okay to treat them. During the pandemic, some businesses didn't believe in the seriousness of the virus and they didn't believe in wearing masks. They didn't believe it made any difference. Their approach to the marketplace was, "We don't believe, so we're not going to comply and we don't care what you believe." You know what? Studies told us that seventy percent of the country thought it did make a difference. These businesses made the choice not to respect seventy percent of the country who believed differently than they believed. They were trying to force their customers to do business their way instead of trying to meet the customer where they were. Seems they forgot who had the money and kept them in business.

You need to meet your customer where they are— not where you want them to be, believe they should be, and not where you are. Where you are doesn't matter in the eyes of the customer. Always play to the customer. I'm not saying the customer is always right. I'm saying that the customer is always right in their own eyes. If you value that customer, you need to be right in the customer's eyes.

The customer is not always right. There are times when the customer is wrong, and I am quick to fire a customer if they are rude or disrespectful in any way. I don't condone rudeness or disrespect so I won't tolerate it from customers just like I won't tolerate it from employees. I speak up and say, "I'd rather not have you as a customer. Let me refer you to one of my competitors who I think deserves you."

My Dog's Name is Leon

A number of companies really do a great job with customer service. I have had excellent service from Chewy, the pet supply company. I buy all of my dog food, pet treats, dog beds, even some of my dog's medicines from Chewy. They're terrific. They're first-class in every way.

When the coronavirus first started and I placed my order with Chewy, they apologized in advance for potential delays in shipping. They explained on their website that they weren't happy with delays, but they were short-handed as a result of the pandemic, and their transportation services had slowed down. They said, "If your order gets there later than usual, please accept our apology in advance. We're doing our very best." I thought, "That's nice. They don't apologize after it's already late. They're apologizing in advance to set me up for what could be disappointing to me when it doesn't arrive like I am used to."

The Chewy website announced, "We're running behind, so give yourself plenty of time." I thought that was a nice touch, but a nicer touch was that the order got there just as it always did. They informed me that I should lower my expectations due to something completely out of their control, then exceeded the expectations. That was either brilliant marketing or great service. And I don't care which one it was, because my products and services got there in a timely way in a great price and all that.

When you do business with Chewy, they ask you your dog's name, birthday, and breed. They load the information into a database then every year on his birthday my bulldog, Leon, gets a birthday greeting via my email. There's that step extra. It costs them nothing. It's a computer program that generates an email. They probably send out hundreds or thousands of these every day, but it's a touch that I remember. That's what customers are looking for: something to set you apart from your competition.

Size Doesn't Matter When It Comes To Doing It Right

There are many companies that do a good job setting themselves apart from their competition. The ones that I like the best are not the great big companies. I expect those companies to get it right—in fact, that's how most of them became great big companies, they do most things right. I always love it when the little guy gets it right. I just love it when the solopreneur goes out of her way to astound me.

I live in Arizona where we have concrete block fences covered in stucco. I wanted to raise mine a couple of blocks higher to add a bit more privacy around my pool. I got a recommendation for a guy to come do the work. He was nice, courteous, and conscientious. Two days after it was all finished and he had been paid, he rang my doorbell. I answered the door and he said, "Are you still happy?"

"You drove over here to ask me if I was happy?" I asked.

"Yes, sir, I did. I want to make sure you're still happy. Let's go look."

We went into the yard and checked it all out and sure enough, I was still happy.

He said, "I think this place right here is a little vulnerable to cracking. I'm going to check back with you in two weeks." He was proactively expecting a problem and telling me not to worry about it because he had it covered.

He was right. I got a little hairline crack that it took a couple of weeks to show up. But I wasn't upset or frustrated or concerned in any way. I didn't even have to call him. He came out all on his own and checked on it and said, "Don't worry, I got it." He patched it up, and said, "I'll come back tomorrow. Set the paint out, and I'll paint it for you."

Here is a guy, all by himself, out there laying blocks and putting on stucco in 115 degrees, and he took the time to come back just to make sure I was happy.

What are the chances of me building another concrete block wall? Not at this house probably. However, with that level of service, I'll make sure I've got his name and his number and I'll tell everybody about him.

Here's another example. In the middle of the coronavirus, I decided that I wanted to convert a little extra bedroom into a dedicated television room with a couple of big leather recliners and a couple of dog beds for my dogs Reba and Leon. Like most people, my wife and I were watching more television during the pandemic and wanted a new, more dedicated spot to kick back and enjoy.

I purchased the television and got it home on my own but I was looking for somebody to hang it, wire it, program it to be compatible with what I already had, hook up the soundbar and fish the cords through the walls. I called a guy who had a nice little website saying that's exactly what he did.

When he answered, he told me who he was and said, "I have some questions for you."

"Really? You have questions for me?"

He said, "Yes, sir. I run my business based on my ratings. How can I make sure I get a five-star rating from you? What can I do to make sure you're going to be happy?"

Wow. He wanted to know in advance what it was going to take to make me happy when he get here and how I would judge whether he had done a good job when he was gone. I said, "The first thing you can do is show up on time."

"Of course, sir," he said. "I would never be late. When we set an appointment, I'll be there on time."

"Thank you. That means a lot to me. I really appreciate that."

He also said, "Sir, we are in a time of pandemic. I wear a mask, and I would appreciate it if you would wear a mask in your own house, too. Will that be okay with you?"

I responded with, "Thank you, because I would require you to wear a mask in my house. So I appreciate your asking that."

We had a great conversation about exactly what I wanted and needed to be done. He quoted a price and then added, "It may vary just by a few dollars if I run into a problem and it takes a little longer."

When he showed up, he was exactly on time. He walked in the door with a vacuum cleaner in his hand.

While I wondered how he was going to hang a television with a vacuum cleaner, I knew this was going to be a good experience because he wanted to clean up his own mess. He drilled the holes, hung the television, ran the wiring, fished the walls, and cleaned up with his vacuum cleaner. He programmed the television to work with my cable and connected the soundbar. Then he went to his truck, brought in spray, and wiped down everything he had touched.

Then he said, "Sir, I would like for you to come in here so we can make sure it's just exactly the way you want it and to see if there is anything else you'd like from me before I leave." I assured him that it all looked great and worked great, too.

Then he said, "Sir, I want to make sure I get a five-star rating, but I want to make sure that I've *earned* that rating by making you completely happy."

"Don't worry," I said, "you're going to get one."

"Is there anything else I can do for you?" he asked.

"As a matter of fact, there is," I said. "I want five business cards. I need to spread your name around when I know someone who can use your services."

He gave me the cards and sent me a follow up email from his truck with the link to leave him a 5 star review. I gave him the review and he sent me a thank you note for doing it. What an outstanding experience and a great example of meeting the customer where they are and setting expectations of excellence, and then doing everything to make sure those expectations are met and exceeded.

When Too Much Of A Good Thing Is A Bad Thing

I collect bourbon. I have over three hundred unique bourbons in my collection. I was at one of my favorite liquor stores to check if they had anything new for my collection. Sure enough, they had something I didn't have. I picked it up and got in line at the register. It was not a short line. It was a line with way too many people in it for me. I hate lines.

The clerk running the register was attempting to build a rapport with each customer who came through the line. I'm just saying to myself, "Lord, please, I just want to give you my money and leave!" But nope, she was determined to be overly-friendly and ask questions that only wasted time. She was friendly, she was wonderful, some folks with nothing better to do were having a great time, but she annoyed the hell out of me. She was providing what she considered to be excellent service by having a conversation with each customer, but she wasn't serving me.

When all I'm doing is paying for a bottle of booze, I'm looking for a fast transaction. I am not looking for a relationship. And when the line is long and people are anxious because of the long wait, conversations don't serve, they do the opposite.

We have to tune in to the way other people want to be treated. They give us visual cues; they give us audible cues. They tell us how they want to be treated. You can set it up like the guy who hung my TV: "How would I know if you've been served well? What would it take to get a five-star review?" You can set up that expectation. But remember, just because that's how you like to do business, that doesn't mean it's how everybody likes to do business.

Customer Service Is Everyone's Job

For solopreneurs it's easier because you only have your own behavior to control. When you have employees, you have to make sure that every single person in the organization contributes to the customer being served well. If you have a brick-and-mortar operation, the person who sweeps the floor and keeps the restroom clean is just as important to overall customer satisfaction as the quality of your product or service or the person who interacts with the customer.

Imagine going to a restaurant where you love their food, but when you walk in, their front door area is full of cigarette butts because nobody has swept them up.

Maybe you even see the employees out front smoking cigarettes. Then you go to the restroom, and it's nasty. Show me a nasty restroom in a restaurant, and I'm convinced that's how the kitchen looks. And in reality that probably really is how the kitchen looks.

The janitor is as important to the customer's experience and perception of quality as any other employee. Now chances are, when we're hiring janitors, we don't explain that to them. We just say, "Here's a dirty bathroom; make it a clean bathroom." Don't be surprised when you get a bad janitor out of that kind of hiring process. The janitor needs to understand that they play a crucial role in customer satisfaction. That's the boss's job to explain.

Every human being that works at the company needs to understand how critical their role is in serving the customer. If they don't understand that, if they don't feel they are a part of serving the customer, don't expect them to serve the customer well, because they don't see that what they do every single day has anything to do with a customer. But every employee has to serve the customer.

Creating Policies for the Few

Sometimes businesses have policies and procedures that are not very customer-friendly and don't make any sense. That happens because these policies are typically created for the few instead of the many. I remember when companies years ago said, "No more personal checks." If you asked the company why they stopped taking personal checks, they would say, "Because checks bounced and we're not able to collect on them or the cost of collecting on them was prohibitive."

Okay, that makes sense. Or does it? What percentage of your customers write bad checks? The truth is, probably less than 1 percent write a bad check. And how many go uncollected? Probably one percent of that one percent, but now you have penalized ninety-nine percent of the people who would never write you a hot check by not allowing them to write you a check at all. Now I am aware that few people write checks today, but how are you doing in your business that keeps the one percent problem fixed by hurting the ninety-nine percent?

There are good customer service policies for sure, but sometimes the policy gets in the way of common sense. Once I was traveling across the country from one coast to the other. It was one of those really tough travel days where nothing was going right. There was no food on any of the flights I was on and because things were running late between flights, there was no time to grab a bite since I was in a mad rush to make my connections.

I'd done the calculations in my mind and I knew I would not arrive at my hotel until about 11:30 p.m. I also knew that room service at this particular hotel chain closed at 11:00, so it was going to be too late for me to get any food. I knew I would be stuck eating out of vending machines in the hallway. I've done it before and it's not the end of the world but it's not my favorite thing to do when I'm really hungry.

Sure enough, around 11:30 p.m. I walk into this particular hotel. Now this is a chain that most people know well. I've told this story many times in my speeches over the years, and I always laughingly say, "I'm not going to tell you the name of the hotel, but I will tell you this: when naming the hotel, there were two trees involved."

Now this particular hotel has a policy whereby the customer gets a cookie upon checking in. I'm standing in line, checking in 11:30 at night, and at the end of registering, the front-desk clerk smiles and says, "Sir, here's your warm chocolate chip cookie." I am so hungry that I grab that cookie and hug it to my chest. I can't wait to get to my room and eat the cookie.

There's a guy right next to me checking in at the same time. He's at the end of his transaction when I hear his front desk clerk say, "Sir, here's your warm chocolate chip cookie."

"No, that's all right," he says. "I'm not really very hungry, and besides, I don't like chocolate."

First of all, I wonder, who doesn't like chocolate? So, I interrupt and say to his clerk, "Excuse me, I'd like that cookie."

"I can't do that, sir," she says. "this cookie has been assigned to *his* room."

"Cookies have room assignments?" I say.

This guy laughs, turns to me, and says, "Hey, hang on a minute, buddy. I'll get you the cookie." He turns back to the clerk and says, "I've changed my mind. I've decided I want the cookie after all."

She says, "I can't do that either, sir. The cookie has already been declined."

That kind of stuff drives me nuts. I know you have seen things just as ridiculous. We all have. Here you have a well-meaning front desk clerk who, I'm sure, had been told that was their policy. I don't know if it really was their policy or one she had dreamed up but I do know that I didn't get that extra chocolate chip cookie that night, because she felt it would be wrong to give another customer's cookie to me.

That policy stood in the way of common sense and customer satisfaction. It also resulted in my telling that story over the years to probably well over a million people. Imagine a million people hearing a customer service story that's not particularly complimentary about your business. And imagine if it was over some silly, well-meaning policy that seemed to make sense on paper but makes no sense in practical application.

Good service comes down to empowering your people with the values you have communicated to them and combing those values with good old common sense. What would it have cost that clerk to give me that chocolate chip cookie? Nothing. I didn't get the cookie because she didn't feel empowered to go against what she thought was the rule, just to do a kind thing for a customer.

If we train our people around our values of serving customers well, solving their problems, alleviating their pain, making them happy, and doing it in a friendly way, they will show their appreciation by coming back again and again. They'll become regulars and might even become advocates.

Every single person in the organization must be empowered to the point where their behavior always exhibits the core values, even if it goes against policy.

Tiny Touches of Thoughtfulness

Nothing beats personal contact. If somebody spends money with me, they deserve a note. Everybody who's ever hired me has gotten a little handwritten postcard from me. I have note cards with my picture on the front. (Nobody wants a picture of me, but still they know it's from me when they open it.) It says, "Thank you for allowing me to serve you. If there is any way I can ever serve you again in the future, please don't hesitate to let me know. Larry Winget." It's three sentences. Three sentences to show appreciation and respect for the customer's time and money. It's not computer generated. It's me, with a pen and paper and a stamp. Personal contact is not hard to make and is more valued than ever in this time of technology where we believe an email or a text is equivalent. It's simply not the same.

Do something that makes business personal again. If you can figure out a way to do that, you're going to find a lot more customer loyalty, because you've improved the experience—and even improved the level of service—in the customer's mind. And you've met the customer literally where they live by dropping them a note. If you don't have the physical address, at a bare minimum drop your customers an email to show your appreciation. People who spend their money want to be shown appreciation for money well spent. They want you to honor their time and money and decision to do business with you.

One of my favorite restaurants called me the day after I had eaten there to make sure that their service was exemplary. That's how they put it: "We want to make sure our service was exemplary."

I say, "Wow! Thanks for the follow-up. Yes, it was."

I'm sure they have some minimum-wage person calling everybody back the day after. That's okay with me. It still made it the experience a bit more personal and tips the scale in their favor when I am making a decision about going there for dinner.

While there are many things you can do, here is what you need to take away from all of this: Do *something*.

Larry's Number One Rule For Life and Business

Do what you said you would do, when you said you would do it, the way you said you would do it.

I believe that sentence sums up what every person ultimately wants. Your customers want you to do what you said you would do. When? When you said you would. How? The way you said you would. It is a statement based in integrity, honesty and respect.

And while your customers want that from you, don't you also want that from your customers? Don't you want your customers to do what they said they would do when they said they would, the way they said they would? Of course you do. You want them to pay you when they said they would don't you?

I believe this statement is exactly what we all want from every other human being, relationship, and business interaction. I want that from my wife; my wife wants that from me. My kids have always wanted that from me as a parent. I've wanted the same thing from my kids. I want everybody I come in contact with to do what they said they would do, when they said they would do it, the way they said they would do it. That's why it is my number one rule for all of life and business. It is rooted in the core values I hold most dear in my life: honesty, integrity, and respect.

8

If You Can't Sell, You Can't Survive

It really is that simple: If you can't sell, you can't be in business. At least not for long that's for sure! Red Motley, one of the original sales trainers from many decades ago, said, "Nothing happens until somebody sells something." I don't care how well you lead, how well you manage, how good your product is, or how well you hire or fire: if you can't get people to pay you money for your product and services, shut your business down and go home.

If you're a solopreneur or you're just starting in business, chances are that you don't have the money to go out and start hiring professional salespeople. Even so, how would you get them to take the job? Oh, wait—you're going to have to sell them on taking the job, so you're still going to have to learn how to sell.

Sell Yourself out of Every Problem

I honestly believe to my core that you can sell yourself out of any problem you have. I've already talked a lot about all the problems you're going to have starting your own business. How are you going to fix those problems? You're going to have to sell your way out of them.

When I was a little boy in Muskogee, Oklahoma, if I was going to have anything, no one was going to give it to me. I was going to have to figure out how to earn my own money so I could buy it. I picked up pop bottles on the side of the road. (That's back when soda was called pop and it came in bottles instead of cans. It was also when people just tossed their bottles out of their car windows into the ditch on the side of the road.) Those bottles were worth 2 cents apiece. I would walk the ditches along the roads for miles to pick them up and sell them to the grocery store for 2 cents each.

We grew lots of strawberries at my house. I would pick strawberries and put them in little baskets and go door-to-door asking people to buy strawberries. We had chickens, so I sold eggs. If it was around and not nailed down, my dad knew I was going to figure out how to sell it so I could have some money.

I grew up understanding the premise that to get money, you had to sell. People make getting money much harder than it really is. There are only two ways to get more money: spend less or earn more. That's all you've got. You can either reduce your expenses to have more of the money you earn, or you can increase your income by earning more money. I have never been particularly great at reducing expenses so the direction that worked best for me was to increase my income. And the fastest way for you to increase your income is to sell your products and services to other people.

How do you sell? Simple: Ask people to buy. Don't complicate it much more than that. Just ask. Ask, ask, ask, ask, ask. You'll be bad at it at first. You will be terrified too. And you will get turned down a LOT. You're not going to get everybody to say yes. Your closing ratio won't be very good at all. If you ask ten people to buy, maybe only one will buy, so your closing ratio is one out of ten. Even if that's as good as you are, you still get to make more money simply by asking more people. If you're only closing one out of ten, go and ask twenty; now you have two sales. Go ask thirty and now you have three sales. Go ask a hundred, and now you have ten. That's all you have to do in order to earn more money: just be willing to ask a lot of people to buy. Along the way, you should get better at asking, so your closing ratio can improve. Then your chances of earning more go up through both quantity and quality. That's a winning combination every time.

My goal as a little boy was to ask every single person who came across my path if they'd like to buy eggs, strawberries, or whatever I had in my hand that day. Later, I worked for Southwestern Bell and AT&T selling telephone systems. I was good at it. When others were struggling to make sales, I was setting records and exceeding my quota. How? I asked everybody, I mean, literally everybody, if they wanted to buy a phone system. If they said no, it didn't hurt my feelings, I'd just go ask the next person. I never considered a "no" to be a personal rejection. I don't believe anybody can reject me; however they do have every right to refuse me. So it didn't bother me when people refused me based on what I was selling. I just moved on to the next person.

If you ask enough people, eventually somebody is going to say yes to you. That was my approach. When I was selling telephone systems, I achieved everything that was expected of me, and then some. Later, when I started my own company selling business telephone systems, I hired people who knew how to ask everybody to buy. I could teach them about the phone systems we were selling, but the most important question about them was whether they had call reluctance. In other words, were they reluctant to pick up the phone and talk to people? Were they reluctant to knock on doors because they felt that every "no" was a personal rejection? Were their feelings hurt because someone said "no" to buying a telephone system? If so, those weren't the people I hired. I hired the ones who would knock on doors, pick up the phone and call all day long saying, "Do you want to buy a phone system?" It was not very sophisticated, but it was very effective.

Later on, after my telephone career and entering the world of professional speaking, I had to sell my own speeches. That wasn't very hard for me because believe it or not, selling speeches is just like selling telephone systems or strawberries. You just ask.

I wrote a lot of sales training material when working for Southwestern Bell and AT&T and I used that training in my own telecommunications company. So when I entered professional speaking, I took that material, packaged it into a number of short sessions, picked up the yellow pages in Tulsa, Oklahoma, and started calling companies. I asked them if their people needed sales training. Sometimes a little print shop might only have one person out on the street selling their printing. That was fine by me as I was more than willing to train them. I was training anybody who needed to know how to sell better regardless of product or service. I taught how to get past the gatekeeper, handle objections, ask for the sale and all of the other components of good selling. I started my professional speaking career as a sales trainer, but later I moved into motivation and business training, and eventually

into what I do today—but at the root of it all is selling. I am selling right here, right now in this book. I'm
offering my products and services and ideas in a way
that relates to your problems as a businessperson and
the pain you are going through or know you will go
through, and I am positioning my ideas as solutions to
those problems in order to alleviate that pain. That's
called *selling*.

Conversations, Not Scripts

Most people who teach sales training are technique
trainers. They teach you snappy ways to start the conversation, or to close the sale, or to deal with objections.
Some of those techniques are effective, but I don't think
they're effective for very long because people are pretty
savvy and can see through them. When people see that
you are using a sales technique on them, they feel manipulated. A person who feels manipulated or hustled by a
sales technique rarely buys.

Technique selling typically revolves around sales
scripts. A script is based on "when the customer says
this, then you say *that*."

The problem is that the customer doesn't have a
script—or at least, they don't have *your* script. The customer rarely says *this* and you are just stuck with all of

that. That won't do much for you if the customer doesn't say the right thing. We have all been on telemarketing calls where it's easy to tell that the person on the other end is following a script and is thrown off because you aren't saying what they desperately need you to say for them to respond correctly.

I've never liked sales scripts. I've never liked memorizing anything. I don't like "pat answers." I like a conversation. In fact, I believe most people enjoy a good conversation. And most love a conversation that is based on making their life or business better and getting their problems solved.

Have more sales conversations. The most interesting thing to people is themselves. If you talk to a customer about what they are going through, if you listen to them and ask questions around what they're going through, how it hurts them and what it costs them to go through it, then you are talking to them about something they are more interested in than in anything else.

People are turned off about selling because they've been badly sold to in the past. They feel like they been hustled, and they probably have. Most people tend to think of selling as a hustle, of taking advantage of someone, of manipulating another person into doing something they don't really want to do and to spend money they don't have. That's not at all what real selling is.

Selling as an Obligation

I believe that selling is an obligation. I see selling my services as something I owe you. If I see that you have a problem—and that problem is causing you pain—it's my obligation to share that solution with you if I have it. If I don't, I'm a bad person because I know what it takes to fix what you're going through and I'm not willing to offer it to you. When people start thinking that selling is an obligation and a matter of serving their customers, then it's not a hustle and it's not manipulation.

Selling is something you do *for* your customer, not *to* your customer.

Customers Don't Care About What You're Selling

I know that's shocking, but it's true. Customers don't really care what you are selling. They care about getting their problem solved. They don't even much care what solves it as long as it gets solved. What does that mean? Get over yourself. You are a minor player in the equation. Make it all about you and you lose. Make it about your product or service and you lose. Make it about the customer and you win.

Recently I went to have my car washed. The salespeople always come out into the lanes where the cars are waiting and do a walkaround. The salesman did his walkaround of my truck, wrote down the kind of wash I wanted to buy and said to me, "We'll throw in a wax for another $19.95. We'll clean out the wheel wells and polish the rims too."

"I'm really not interested today," I said. "I'm really on a short time frame and don't have time for it. I might do that next time." I was doing everything I could to politely but clearly put him off because I just didn't want to mess with it, but he wouldn't give up. Finally, I said, "I don't want to mess with any of this. Stop selling me because I'm not buying."

"Sir," he said, "that's really not fair. Do you understand that I make my money based on selling these services?"

I said, "Let me stop you right there and do a little sales training for you. Don't tell me I'm not fair. I'm always fair. I'm the customer. I can't be anything but fair, especially when I'm being polite to you. Secondly, I don't care about what gets you paid. That is none of my business. You trying to sell me a wax job and a wheel cleaning should be about me and making me happy, not about the fact that you get compensated for it. You've just put you and your money ahead of me and what I'm interested in."

One more time to be clear: People buy for their reasons, not for your reasons. People only spend money to solve a problem. They never spend money to solve a problem you believe they have; they only spend money to solve a problem *they* believe they have.

Salespeople need to clearly understand that the customer doesn't care how much money you make or if you even make any money. Customers care about themselves and their problems, not about you and your problems.

When entrepreneurs get over themselves, and leading with their ego, and begin thinking with the mind of a customer, they will start to be successful.

The main thing any entrepreneur should get out of their mind is that they matter. I know that's a shock to some people. But if you get that out of your mind, you will be much better off and will make a whole lot more money. When you start to think like a customer—like you are spending your own money—you will get really selfish and picky about how you spend that hard earned money, and that's when the customer will share that money with you and your business.

Sales Malpractice

Too many salespeople say something like, "Look, I've got *this*. You want *this*, don't you? Why wouldn't you want something as cool as *this*?" Yep, that's their pitch. Pay attention next time someone is trying to sell you something. That's about as deep as it goes.

It's like going on LinkedIn, where the instant you accept a connection with somebody, you get a message from that person telling you how you've just got to have this cool thing they offer. I got one the other day saying, "Thank you so much for connecting. Larry, I would like to set up a meeting with you so I can talk to you about how you can write a bestselling book and get on lots of media."

I wrote back and said, "I've written six *New York Times* and *Wall Street Journal* best sellers, I'm a regular on many national television shows, and I've had my own television show. You should have qualified your client list much better before asking me to buy something when you haven't determined that I have a need for it." And you know what? They got mad at me because I pointed out the incompetence of their sales efforts. Then I gave them a little lesson on what they should have said. They should have paid me for that lesson. They didn't.

Every day people are offering solutions to problems that are not yet identified. The connection with a potential customer shouldn't be made around your product or service. The connection with a customer should be made around the problem someone is going through. People will do anything to solve the problem and to avoid the pain it causes. If you tap into that fact, then your product or service will seem cheap to them—and you're not selling, you're serving people by solving their problems and alleviating their pain.

At this point in the book you should be sick of me talking about the customer's problem and the pain that causes it. I know I'm sick of saying it. But I'm even more sick of people who don't understand this basic principle of business. It's why people fail. It's why people are broke. It's why they lose their business and end up disappointed and probably bankrupt. It's also why some people get rich and do amazing things. It's all there is. If you don't solve a problem, then you don't have a business. If you don't talk to the customer about their problem, then you are not interesting to them. Understanding this is what keeps you from becoming a commodity. So, forgive the broken record and learn this lesson!

Often Over-Looked But Essential Sales Tools

The Power of Friendliness

I recently read a study that said people are looking for friendliness now more than ever simply because we've lost a lot of it in our society. Look at any social media site and you will know that's a fact. We don't see a lot of nice and friendly anymore. We see vitriolic, hateful, and mean. That's the world we are surrounded with right now, so when we see friendliness, we are attracted to it like a magnet.

In business, friendly wins. Being likable wins. When people are friendly and likable, you want to be around them.

There are many times I have paid more and sacrificed things that I originally thought to be important simply because I really liked the salesperson, which built trust. You've done the same thing. Knowing that people are looking at those qualities as a reason to do business with you means that you should consciously go out of your way to be more likable and friendly. That might be a challenge for some!

Look Successful

I'm always amazed when I go on a Zoom call for business and somebody looks as if they have just fallen out of bed. They haven't combed their hair, haven't put on their makeup, and haven't put on a nice shirt or top. "Well, we're just online here, Larry," A friend of mine told me the other day. I said, "Really? How disrespectful of you to think that I'm not worth having you comb your hair or putting on a nice shirt." Yep, I said it. Would you?

I was able to jokingly rough up my friend a little bit over this, but people make this same mistake when they're talking to their clients. I want to do business with someone who looks successful. I want them to represent the success they say they have in selling me their product or service. If you look like a bum, I'm going to think you're a bum. If you use bad grammar, I'm going to think you're dumb.

If you don't do what it takes to make sure your messaging is spelled right or is grammatically correct, then guess what? I'm not going to trust you with my business or my money. I'm not going to trust that you are smart enough or care enough to solve my problem.

That's the way it really is. Look successful. Look smart. Make sure that your website looks like it belongs to a successful person. Make sure that everything that represents you looks good. You are judged by everything you put out there. Everything. Every social media post, every text and every email exchange. Every interaction with the public gives the marketplace a reason to judge your competence.

People say, "Well, you know the Bible says, 'Judge not, lest ye be judged.'" People love to throw that Bible verse at me. Actually the Bible says, "Do not judge, or you too will be judged. For in the same way you judge others, you will be judged, and with the same measure you use, it will be measured to you." (Matthew 7:1–2 NIV). I'm willing to be judged by the same measure. I'm willing for you to judge the success of my business by the quality of the work I put out. We judge every time we vote for somebody, every time we go to one grocery store over another, every time we pick one dry cleaner and not another. Those are judgments.

Everything you put out there—what you say, how you say it, how it is spelled, how it is grammatically put on paper, even how you combed your hair this morning will be judged. Why not stack the deck in your favor by doing your best?

Be Informed

Sometimes when I'm talking to someone about their industry and I tell them there was just a story about what they do in *Forbes* or *The Wall Street Journal* they will reply, "Hmm. I didn't know that." How can they not know what is going on in their industry? It's because they are not reading anything. They are not paying attention to what's going on in the world. They are not seeing buying trends, they haven't been to the mall, they don't know anything about the economy or new governmental regulations. They don't belong to their trade association and they don't watch what their competitors are doing and how they are doing it. If you're going to be successful, you have to have your thumb on the consumers' pulse.

When entrepreneurs start to experience a little success, they become laser-focused. A lot of experts say that being laser-focused is the key to becoming successful, and in some ways that is correct. But you can become so laser-focused that you stop paying attention to what's going on in the marketplace and live in a bubble that leaves you painfully uninformed and ignorant.

I was talking to my fashion designer son recently, and he rattled off the names of about twenty-five companies that had just filed for bankruptcy. He was reciting detailed information from many business articles. I said, "Wow, Son, you really have studied this."

"Dad, this is my business," he said. "If I don't know what others are doing, I won't know how to react and respond to the marketplace quickly enough, so it doesn't happen to me."

That's paying attention to what's going on in the world instead of sitting back and saying, "What do you know? Look at all those companies going out of business. I had no idea. I wonder why?" All you have to do is spend a few minutes every day paying attention to the marketplace and doing a little bit of research. That can save you tons of money and maybe save your company in the process.

Listen

The customer has all of the information you need to make the sale. The marketplace has all of the information you need to be successful. Mentors, coaches, and folks smarter than you have lots of great information that you can use to excel in every area of both life and business. In order to take advantage of that information, you have to shut up and listen. If you don't shut up, pay attention, and listen to what is going on around you, the information will pass you by. And that information is being heard by your competition.

Listening is not just being quiet so the other person can finish what they're saying and you can go back to talking. Make sure you're a good listener as well as an active one. Read about listening and what that really means. Practice listening with someone who you don't care one bit about what they have to say. That is the greatest practice of all. And it's a challenge. But when you learn to listen to information you don't care about, you will get better at listening when it's something important. Besides, listening to someone whether you agree with them or not, is a form of respect.

Practice listening to little kids. Practice listening to your husband, your wife or your significant other. Listen to them, and then summarize what they said: "From what you're telling me, this is what I understand." Otherwise, you're never going to be any good at listening to your customers.

If there is anything that irritates me (and there is much, I can assure you), it's having to repeat myself because the other person is so involved in what they are doing they don't hear what I've said. I have stood at the counter in a fast-food restaurant after the clerk has asked me for my order and said, "I'll have the cheese-burger with mustard, no onions, an order of fries and a small Coke."

Their response is, "Okay, what was it again?" I then repeat, and they say something like, "You want fries with that?"

I say, "Yes, I still want fries with that."

"What do you want to drink?"

"I still want a small Coke." I reply.

It's frustrating almost beyond words to me that they didn't care enough the first time I said it, to bother listening to me. And their boss should observe that behavior and fix it. Learn to listen. Teach the people who work for you to listen. It's a basic interpersonal skill.

Circulate to Percolate

There's an old saying: you've got to circulate to percolate. That means that you've got to get out there among the people. You've got to start showing up where potential customers congregate and letting them know what you do and what problems you solve. You can't hide and expect for your business to flourish.

If you have a business, you need a YouTube channel so you can shoot a video that lasts for two or three minutes maybe every day or so and say, "Hello, my name is, and I own this, and this is what I do for a living, and this is the problem it solves." Spend a few minutes educating the marketplace about what they're going through and your solutions. Become a resource in the eyes and minds of people so when they recognize the problem you solve, you will be the person they turn to for a solution.

You need to go places where buyers are, and where your competitors congregate. Belong to your professional trade association. Belong to and attend Chamber of Commerce functions. Get involved in community affairs. People will start to say, "That's the person who does this or that." "That's the person who owns a dry cleaner." "That's the person who coaches personal responsibility." You've got to be someone that others recognize as an expert in your field. And you can't do that if you stay hidden and rely on your website to do your work for you.

Social media is a great way to accomplish these goals. Just be careful and don't totally rely on social media to do what some good old face-to-face networking will do. People still do business with people, so get some personal contact going.

Beware The Charlatans

Many people claim to be experts on any number of issues. How do I know they're experts? They said so. Their social media page told me they were. Their website said they were.

The language of the Internet is hyperbole

"I'm the biggest." "I'm the best." "I'm the world's greatest." The truth is, that can't be proven. A new author wrote me recently asking for a cover quote for her new book. In the book's preface she claimed that the book was a "ground-breaking book in the world of personal development." I wrote back and told her that before she said her book was "groundbreaking" she needed to prove that she had broken ground. All she had done was repackage a bunch of worn out old motivational clichés around her boring person story. I didn't give her the cover quote and I am sure she will continue to promote her book as groundbreaking.

Sadly, because of the internet, we get to say whatever we want to about ourselves, and we are rarely challenged for it. I see people who claim to be bestselling authors, even though their book has never hit an accredited list and is rated at nine million on Amazon. I saw the website of a new speaker recently with a picture of her on stage in front of a huge crowd with her receiving a standing ovation. A closer look told me that she had photoshopped herself onto that stage. If I could see it, buyers could see it.

When people make outrageous claims, be skeptical. Verify. Do some research. Especially if you are thinking of spending money with them. Believe it or not, people will lie to you about their accomplishments.

You also need to be careful about what you say about yourself and your accomplishments. Don't exaggerate. Don't be guilty of hyperbole. Eventually that stuff will catch up with you and cost you dearly.

The Five Reasons People Don't Buy

Allow me to give you a short course on why people don't buy. I wish I could take credit for these five reasons and give credit where credit is due, but the truth is that I just don't remember where I first heard these five points. In any case, I am not claiming originality here, but I am going to put my own spin on this concept.

Five Reasons People Don't Buy:

• No need

• No hurry

• No money

• No want

• No trust

No need. As I've already pointed out, people rarely buy what they need, and if they really need it, they'll figure out how to buy it without involving anybody else. People buy what they want, which is much more important.

No hurry. This one is about slowing the salesperson down to postpone having to make a decision. Sometimes it's because the customer just doesn't have the ability to be succinct and say no. You've probably heard something like, "This is really good, and I'm really interested, but I've got to check with my wife." Or "Let me get back to you." Or "The next time I want something, I'll remember you." That's postponement. There's no sense of urgency to move ahead now.

You know why there's no sense of urgency? They don't feel the pain enough to want to solve the problem. So again, what's your job? Go back to the pain point. "If I understood you correctly, you said you were going through this, and you don't like to go through that. When you do, it costs you in these ways. If I were you, I know I would want to move past that pain as quickly as I possibly could, and I'm sure you want to do the same thing. Is this a problem you're willing to spend the money to solve? Does this hurt badly enough that you're willing to invest in a solution? Or are you just irritated enough to talk about the problem without really fixing it?" When you do that, you will establish whether the prospect is really willing to spend the money to fix the problem or not. You will create a sense of urgency for them. Even if they decide not to buy, you'll have a clearer picture of their thinking about you as a solution.

No money. People will lie to you about their money more than any other topic. In fact, when it comes to money, you rarely get the truth from anyone. They claim to have money when they are so broke they can't pay attention. They claim to be broke when they've got more than enough to buy whatever they want.

"No, I can't afford to do that right now," doesn't necessarily mean they really can't afford it. People will use a lack of money as an excuse more than any other excuse. Yet we all know this fact: If you want something badly enough, you will find the money to get it.

Again, I want to remind you of your job. Your job is to make people want your product or service badly enough that they will move heaven and earth to get it. How do you do that? Remind them of the problem they are trying to solve and the pain in causes them.

No want. As I've said many times already, "Find out what people want and give them more of it. Find out what they don't want, and don't give them any of that." You have to figure out what people want. Notice that I did not say that you've got to know what people *need*. You think you know what people need, but people rarely buy what they *need*. They always buy what they *want*. If they need it, they'll figure out a way to buy it.

Toilet paper is something people need. We don't have a lot of toilet paper salespeople in this world because people will just go out, find it, and buy it. They'll take care of that basic need. Think a toilet paper salesperson is required? Do you remember the toilet paper shortage at the beginning of the pandemic? People were willing to pay a ton of money for a fat roll of double-ply.

I have gone to the mall because I needed to buy a new pair of black shoes, and I've come home with a putter. I needed those black shoes, but I wanted that new putter, and the putter won out. The putter will win every single time.

There are many ways to discover customer wants and needs. Google is amazing. You can get on your computer, type in just about any question you can imagine and find an answer. You can discover buying trends, marketing trends, sales trends, trends by geographic location, by age, and more. You can spend a few minutes on your computer and you will know what the marketplace is demanding and what your competitors are doing to supply that demand. It takes very little time or effort.

I was recently coaching a new speaker who wanted to speak to nurses and told me that she couldn't find any groups of nurses to speak to. While on the phone complaining to me about the lack of opportunity, I did a Google search and came up with lists of nursing associations in the United States. There are several hundred national, state and local associations of nurses. I asked how many of these she had contacted. None. She said she wasn't aware of them and didn't know where to look to find them.

Many entrepreneurs go into business because they are convinced there is a need for their product or service. When people bring me an idea for which they say there's a need in the marketplace, I always say to them, "Okay, there is a need, but is there a *desire* in the marketplace? Is there a *want* in the marketplace?"

Do people want the product enough to spend money on it, or do they just want it? There's a lot of stuff I want, but I don't want it badly enough to buy it. So, the question is always going to be, "Do they want it badly enough to spend their money, give you their credit card number, write you a check, or pull out their big stack of $100 bills? Do they want it that much? Or is it just something you believe they need or should want?"

No trust. People don't do business with people they don't trust. They don't do business with big institutions they don't trust and this gets proven weekly. When a company does something that violates the trust of the people stock prices plummet and the masses boycott the product or the company.

Let me give you a couple of overlooked ways that you can destroy trust: Tell me you'll be there at 10:00 and show up at 10:30. I don't trust you anymore.

I wanted some big, fancy, wooden garage doors, and had arranged for a person to meet me at my house to sell me two sets. I had done my research, knew which doors I wanted, knew the price and this was basically a formality for writing it all up. The salesperson had an appointment set for 10:00 a.m. He wasn't there at 10:00. At 10:30, he rang my doorbell and said he was there to write up the contract for the doors as planned. I said, "You can go ahead and leave because I won't be buying doors from you."

"Why?"

"You're thirty minutes late."

"It's only thirty minutes."

"When did you know you were going to be late? I mean, exactly at what point did you know you were going to be late?"

"When I went out of my first job this morning, I saw it was going to take longer. That was about 8:30."

"That's when you should have called me. If you had called me at 8:30, saying, 'I'm not going to be able to make the 10 a.m. appointment, but I can push it till 10:30; will that still be all right?' I would still have trusted you. But because you didn't bother to call me, you disrespected me. I no longer trust that you can put the garage doors in in a way that's going to satisfy me, because I can't trust you to keep your word even when it comes to showing up at the appointed time."

"I don't think that's fair."

I laughed and said, "Of course it's fair, I'm the customer."

Then I handed him a postcard with my picture on it that said, "Do what you said you would do, when you said you would do it, the way you said you would do it." He turned around and walked away.

Now some people might say, "Larry, you're being awfully picky." You are damn right I'm being picky. It's my money, and I don't share my money willy-nilly with people I don't trust because they can't be bothered with keeping their word.

Build Trust With Value

Ever had a conversation like this before?

"The product costs $3,000."

"I don't have $3,000," or "I don't want to spend $3,000."

"Tell you what I'm going to do for you. Because we're in the middle of a global pandemic, I'm going to sell the product to you for $2,299."

"Wait. A minute ago, it was $3,000. If I'd had the $3,000, you'd have taken it, wouldn't you?"

"Yes, of course I would."

"But because I gave you a little pushback, you just lowered the price by $700."

"I knew that you were a little reluctant."

"Actually, then it costs $2,300. I tell you what: it's still too much money."

"Well, I might be able to get it down to $1,999."

"Look at you lowering the price. I don't trust you now, for sure, about the value of your product or your service."

Lowering your price does not build trust; it destroys trust.

In a selling situation, if you ever get pushback around price and you find yourself being defensive about it then it's because you don't understand your value. Don't defend your price; establish your value.

Always go back to the problem, the pain, what it costs them, and establish your value by addressing what they're going through but will no longer have to go through if they take advantage of your product or service. But whatever you do, don't lower your price the first time you get pushback because it destroys trust.

So no need, no hurry, no money, no want, and no trust. Those are the five reasons people don't buy and the biggest reason is always going to be trust. People buy when they trust, and *never* buy when they don't trust.

Do The Right Thing Even When It Costs You Money

I was remodeling my kitchen recently, and the contractor made a mistake when installing the plumbing. The mistake didn't show up until after the wood floor was installed and all the cabinets were in, the painting was done, and the appliances were set. In other words, until it was all finished. A small leak happened in the ceiling that ruined the floor, the baseboards, some of the drywall and required that it all be replaced. It was a mess in every sense of the word and a huge inconvenience for me, the homeowner, who was trying to live in the mess.

This small problem was an expensive mistake for my contractor. However, he didn't gloss over it or blame anyone else. He could have blamed the plumber or the drywall guy; he could have done a lot of things. Instead, he simply said, "I need to apologize to you both. This leak has happened and I'm not going to put it off on anybody else. This is going to take a couple of weeks to fix. It's going to be a mess. The floor has to be ripped up and the appliances pulled, and the drywall replaced. It's going to cost me a lot of money, but it's going to cost you some time. And Larry, I know your time is more important to you than anything else, and you don't like the disruption. I'm sorry, and here's what I'm going to do to fix it."

I was disappointed and frustrated, but I appreciated the honest, responsible approach. He recognized my concerns and went straight to the ugly, "I messed up. Here's what I'm going to do to fix it, and here's the time frame for fixing it. Here's what you can expect."

We all appreciate someone who's honest with us even when the truth is ugly. Even when the truth is expensive. Even when the truth is hard to tell and a lie is easier, never lie. If you would lie to me about the little things, you would lie to me about the big things.

Overselling

Have you ever been oversold? Of course, you have. It's when a salesperson doesn't know when to quit. They have been told one of those stupid motivational clichés about how winners never quit or that failure is not an option, and they keep pounding away even though it's not paying off for them.

I am all for being persistent, but it has to be appropriate persistence. When persistence becomes inappropriate, it's just flat out annoying and bothersome.

When you constantly bother a client with your sales message, it is evident that it's all about you and not about them or their problem. And the minute the sales process becomes about you, you lose. There is a fine line between showing your interest in solving the customer's problem, and being so obvious that all that can be seen is your interest in making a buck.

When all the customer can think about when they see a text, email, or phone call from you is, "Oh no, please no, not them again!" Then you've gone too far. And it proves you don't listen. And it's evidence that you lack savvy. And respect. And common sense. And it is evidence you don't get that no really does mean no.

If the customer has made it clear that he is really not going to buy from you, then do the right thing and say thank you and move on down the road. Let the customer rest for a while. Maybe a long while before going back to them. Maybe they felt undue pressure from you. Maybe they realized that they really don't have the money. Maybe their problem really isn't so significant that they want to spend the money on solving it. Maybe they just don't want to do business with you, and they don't want to tell you the truth about it. Maybe they just don't like you.

Here's the nice thing about selling: there's always another customer. There is always someone else having the problem that you and your product and service solve. Find them and ask them to buy. You don't have to sell to every single customer; you just need to sell to the next one, and the next one, and the next one.

Stop trying to convince others

By now, you should see that every aspect of business success is based on selling.

Notice that I didn't say *convincing*. I don't believe in convincing people of anything. I am not a convincer. However, I do believe in laying out your case in such a way that people can't say no to you. Your goal is to become impossible to say no to. You do that by laying out your argument in such a way that it makes so much sense that there's nothing the other person can say but yes. They can't say no to you without looking silly. Sound impossible? It's not. When you make so much sense that yes is the only possible answer that makes sense to them, they will stop saying no to you. That means you understand their problem and their pain and how your product or service solves the problem and alleviates their pain. When they are willing to solve the problem because the cost of having the problem is more than the cost of solving it, and you ask them to buy, it will be impossible for them to say no.

9

What to Do When It All Goes to Hell (And It Will)

What a chapter title, huh? Not very optimistic, for sure. But that's the real situation for most entrepreneurs and small businesses. That's why I like the title. A lot. I like it because it is something that too few are prepared for. We teach people how to be successful. Part of our culture has evolved into the idea that things can only go well. We expect a tidy little bow to appear at the end of every situation and to seal it all with a happy-face sticker. It's almost as if we are hiding our heads in the sand and are trying to convince ourselves that the only direction is up. No, there is also down. And as I made perfectly clear at the beginning of this book, down is the way most business ventures go. That is reality. So, you have to be prepared for it. We do little to prepare people for what to do when it all goes to hell. Here is some simple advice.

The Emotions Of Crisis

Whenever something goes wrong, you will experience a variety of emotions. These emotions are natural. Loss or failure isn't easy to deal with and you are going to have to deal with the feelings that are created. I suggest that you read *On Grief and Grieving* by Elisabeth Kübler-Ross, where she talks about the Five Stages Of Grief: denial, anger, bargaining, depression, and acceptance.

When your business isn't going well, your first go-to will be denial. You will do your best to convince yourself that it's not as bad as it appears. And you will be right, it's not as bad—it's worse. Customers don't trust you or your product or service so they don't buy from you. You don't know what you're doing. Your product doesn't solve a problem people are willing to spend money to solve. You started too soon without enough capital to last. And the list goes on and on. But chances are high that you will deny the ugly truth and blame the stupidity of the customers instead of yourself. You will deny that the problem is real and you will continue to bang your head against the wall.

Your results won't change and you will get mad about it. How dare people not see how amazing you are?

What's wrong with the market anyway? Your anger will show up with your customers, your suppliers and then it will slip over into your personal life. Let me save you some time: Get mad right now but be mad at yourself. You caused this mess. Don't blame anyone else. Get mad, then get off your butt and go to work to fix it!

But you probably won't get mad at yourself. Instead, you will start to wheel and deal with yourself. That's the bargaining step. You will make a deal with God or the devil just to get out of the mess you are in. This is a dangerous step for an entrepreneur. This is when you are vulnerable to the charlatans of self-help and business coaching. You will sell your soul and all of your possessions searching for the key to success. You will create a sad, horrible story to gain the pity of others and do your best to find a deep meaning as to why you are failing.

Now you feel worthless. That's the depression. Been there, done that. I lost it all and felt horrible. A natural response for anyone. After all, it was my fault. Feeling like crap was just part of taking responsibility. Knowing you made the mess can be very depressing. So, I'm okay with a little personal responsibility making you feel like crap. For a while. I know each of these emotions are natural for most types of loss from death to divorce to business failure. So to skip them is just putting them off. Recognize them, feel them, give them all a moment and use them to move on.

Move on to the acceptance phase. That doesn't mean that you give up, it means that you take a realistic look at the problem or situation and accept it for what it is. If it's a mess, admit it's a mess. What do you do when faced with a mess? If the mess is that you dropped a box of cereal and it all spilled out, then you probably got a broom and a dust pan or maybe a vacuum and cleaned it up. You didn't stand there frozen, looking at the mess and wringing your hands. You didn't deny that the cereal was all over the floor. You saw it and dealt with it by accepting it for what it is. That's what you do in business, too.

But at some point, you have to be able to say, "Stop." Emotions make a bad boss and none of us should ever turn over the supervision of our life or our business to our emotions. Acknowledge the emotions, and then get to work.

You've got to kick into action! Your business is under attack, your family is under attack, your finances are under attack. You are about to lose everything! You've got to learn to fight back. You've got to be nimble and quick. You have to move like greased lightning so you don't fall further behind while you're regrouping.

Change Is Coming

In 1962, Sam Walton opened his first Walmart store in Bentonville, AR. Over the next thirty years he expanded and moved into every state. And your average small business found themselves in trouble. When I first started in the speaking business, there were a lot of speakers teaching what to do when Walmart comes to town. Small businesses were failing in small towns across America, because they couldn't compete from a pricing standpoint with Walmart, who could buy a million of something when the average small business was buying a couple of dozen.

However, a lot of people figured out how to weather the storm and survive the business "pandemic" that many considered Walmart to be. They "discovered their uniqueness and learned to exploit it in the service of others" and they survived. Many realized that customers still wanted to do business with friendly faces they had known for years.

Now, let's look at Walmart and what happened to them and all the other retailers in America. The Internet came to town and Amazon came to the Internet.

I can buy just about anything I want, and it will be here by tomorrow. Sometimes by this afternoon! From groceries to lawn mowers to live plants—you name it and all I have to do is click a button, and within a few hours, it's sitting on my doorstep. If I don't like it, all I have to do is hit another button that says "return" and with very little effort and lots of options of how to go about it, it's gone! It's amazing. And the best part? I don't have to deal with some surly clerk ignoring me while they ring me up. I only have to deal with my ability to click a button.

Walmart happened to small retailers and Amazon happened to Walmart. What did Walmart do? They responded with their own online shopping system in order to compete. And now we see lots of businesses converting to online retail in a big way as a result of Amazon. Amazon changed the way we shop. Smart businesses came up with online opportunities for their customers to do business with them. The marketplace changed as a result of an outside influence that many considered to be a horrible business crusher for entrepreneurs and small businesses. Now small businesses are being created and are thriving for the very reasons they once went out of business. But there is more change ahead. Jeff Bezos recently said, "I predict one day Amazon will fail. Amazon will go bankrupt. If you look at large companies, their lifespans tend to be thirty-plus years, not a hundred-plus years."

Hard to imagine isn't it? But very forward thinking of Bezos to realize that and to accept it. What's the next thing going to be? I don't have a clue. Neither do you. But if you are going to compete then you've got to be nimble, quick, and willing. Willing is hard. If you are not willing to keep up and change the way you do business and relate to the marketplace, you will become extinct.

Survival of the Fittest

Business adversity is not a bad thing. We have a tendency to feel sorry for those who can't run a successful business. I don't have that tendency. I am typically pretty happy to see a poorly run business go away. I know that when it happens it is more than likely because they were not good at being in business and didn't serve customers well. Or they were poorly run with bad management. And now they are gone and there is more room for good businesses that have figured out what it takes to serve customers well. Plus, when a bad business fails it saves me from wasting my time and money helping that happen!

Adversity has a way of weeding out the businesses that were already poorly run, in a declining market, or undercapitalized. This is much like the Darwinian principle of survival of the fittest. Darwin's principle suggest that organisms best adjusted to their environment are the most successful in surviving and reproducing. Seems fair to me when it comes to business as well as a species: Adjust to the changing environment or go the way of the dinosaur.

In 2008 when the financial crisis hit, the speaking industry was flourishing. In a matter of just a year, the speaking industry was cut to probably less than half of what it had been simply because most speakers couldn't figure out how to stay in business unless times were good and opportunities were plentiful. That was actually good for the speakers who knew what they were talking about, had good marketing, responded well to serving their customers, and had built up their credibility so people could rely on them and trust them for solid content and value. It was a matter of natural selection and survival of the fittest. The others weren't fit, so they didn't survive. I don't really feel bad about those folks. They had the same opportunities to become fit as the rest of us, but weren't willing or were just too lazy to do so. So, bye.

Typically when things are really good, a lot of people get into business, because it's not hard to be successful when everybody's successful. You became successful in a booming economy. Okay, big deal. The question is, "Were you lucky, or were you good?" You really show what you're made of when you're successful even though everything is falling apart around you. If you can succeed when things suck, you've done something.

Maybe You Deserve To Fail

Everybody plans for success. Few people plan for failure. Our entire society is based on preparing people to be successful. School only teaches kids how to be successful. (And that statement is a stretch at this point, I know!) We don't spend nearly enough time teaching people what to do when it all goes to hell and they experience failure. When you never deal with disappointment and have been saved from it at every turn, you aren't equipped to handle it when it comes along. When from kindergarten on you get a trophy for just showing up, the emotions you will experience when things don't go to your way can be devastating. We tell people they can do anything, but the truth is, they can't. We tell them they deserve the best in every way, when in reality, maybe they deserve to go out of business.

The number one reason companies fail is they deserve to fail. They weren't serving their customers. They didn't build a business that was based on solving customers' problems. They didn't create a reputation for being of value to others. Maybe they got into business when everybody had lots of money and the economy was great. People were spending money right and left and you could sell true crap and still make a pretty good living. But when money gets tight, and things get tough, crap doesn't sell. Quality, service, friendliness, solving customer problems, meeting customer needs, alleviating customer pain—that's what keeps you in business.

Circle the Wagons

When I was a little boy growing up in the late fifties and sixties, I loved Westerns. I still love Westerns. In every

Western where there was a wagon train involved, the wagon train was eventually attacked. The first thing you heard the wagon master yell was, "Circle the wagons!"

Why did they put the wagons in a circle? So they could put their resources in the middle and keep them safe from the attackers on the outside of the circle. In the old Westerns, they put their guns and ammunition, food and other resources on the inside, because they wanted to protect them.

You have to do the same thing in your business when it is being attacked. Assess your resources to decide what is most precious to you and what you need to protect. Which employees are you going to put in the middle of the circle? In the old days of the wagon trains, they put women and children in the middle and put the ones who could fight close to the rim of the circle for the battle. When it comes to employees, you've got to decide which folks you want in the middle of the circle to protect and which you want on the front lines to fight.

By the way, the pandemic has been a benefactor in terms of employee evaluation. Employers were quick to discover who they needed in the middle and who would help defend them against their attackers in the marketplace. It was also a gift in helping businesses figure out who they could live without completely. If they aren't worth protecting for life "after the attack" and they aren't any good at fighting off the attack, then let them go now as they are just in the way and using up precious resources.

In the old Westerns, they would assess the talents of each person. "You grab a rifle, you're on the front line." "You make sure we're well fed." "You make sure that the guns are loaded and ready to fire." "You make sure everybody's got ammunition." "You are the look out. You spot anybody who's coming to attack us." "You sound the alarm." People had their talents assessed and were assigned responsibilities accordingly. All of those elements fall into our businesses today.

When my telecommunications business was in trouble, everybody became front line sales people. Technicians and installers sold spare phones and battery backup systems. Everyone in the company was assessed according to their skills and we capitalized on those skills.

Assess the other resources that you've put in the center of the circle. How much ammunition do you have? In other words, what products do you have on hand right now that you could sell? What services could you provide right now that you never even thought of, that you could be offering to people to earn quick money? If you'll remember an earlier statement I made that you can sell yourself out of almost any problem in business, you will be more likely to make it. But you've got to have something to sell and then get out there and ask people to buy it.

You also need to know whom to call for help, and when. When unable to handle the attackers with their own resources, the wagon train had to send somebody out through the attackers to send word so the cavalry or other help could come to the rescue. You may need help too. Don't be so egotistical that you think you can always do it on your own. It's okay to ask for help. It doesn't make you weak to recognize you aren't equipped to go it alone and that you need to bring on other resources. In fact, it's a sign of strength. There are business coaches that are great resources. There's wonderful information online and terrific books that can advise you what to do when everything has gone to hell. Ask for help. Look for help. Accept the help and take advantage of the help.

Remember that you can't just start looking for help when you're in the middle of crisis. I suggest you establish some of these resources ahead of the crisis as a "just in case." You need to constantly be building a network of reliable people who can count on you and whom you can count on, so when things go bad you will have somebody you can call.

Don't be afraid to pay for help. Typically, advice is worth what you pay for it. A lot of people on the inside of your circle will be telling you how you did it wrong and what you could have done differently. That's fine. Learn from them too when they have something of value to offer. But that free advice was worth what you paid for it. Go to the people who are true experts and have built a reputation based on their solid advice. They can save you a lot of time even though they cost you some money.

Assess your provisions so that you know how much money you have set aside. Assess the talent that is still there with you inside the circle. Assign specific tasks to ensure you are using all of the talent in the best way. Call on experts for help and be willing to pay them what they are worth to help you. Then double down on your efforts. Work every minute. Never lay your weapons down, because the second attack always comes when you are least prepared. I know because I've seen the movie!

Learn from every battle you fight so you can improve your skills for the next one. It would be a waste to think that the information here only applies only to a single crisis. These principles will work in every crisis. We didn't need a global pandemic to happen for you to know you should have been saving more money. You can't afford to wait to assess the people who are with you before things get tough. You need to know what your provisions are now, not after it's happened. You need to know what everybody's individual talent is and how to play to their strengths. You need to decide who is dead wood and who isn't contributing now, not when you are out of money and can't afford to pay them.

That's what circling the wagons is about: having a plan that you can rely on every time things go to hell.

That's what my wife, Rose Mary, and I have been so good at for the last forty years. When something bad happens, we know what to do. Yes, we go through all of the normal emotions like everyone else does. But whether it's death, sickness, financial issues, family or relationship problems, business setbacks or any other attack of any type, we go into "circle the wagons" mode. We have done it so many times, that it has become natural to us. We know our roles and our strengths and we can go in defense mode in a femtosecond. As a result, we have survived four decades of ups and downs and attacks.

So don't think this advice is just for your business, this is also life advice and the principles are worth taking note of.

When Should You Get Out?

So, you've given it your best and it just isn't working out. You've circled the wagons, fought like hell. Called in the experts. Sold your soul and everything else you can get money for and there doesn't appear to be any answer.

Here is the popular advice: Never give up! I know that you've heard that advice. It's stupid advice. Much advice that is consider popular is. If you've tried everything and nothing is working, give up. Try something else but give up what isn't working. And if none of it is working, then give it all up! Seriously, just quit. Don't go any more into debt chasing a rabbit that is too far down the hole.

"But Larry! Failure is not an option!" Another popular and stupid saying. Failure is always an option. It was an option when you started. In fact, it was a likelihood. Grieve it and accept it.

I see too many entrepreneurs who are so passionate about their dream that their emotions have gotten in the way of their good sense and they hang on too long. They keep borrowing money from their spouse or from their family, or they go to the bank or the government to fix their cashflow problems when in reality all they are doing is prolonging the inevitable. A short term influx of cash to get you "over the hump" probably isn't the long-term solution that will save your business.

Don't keep going deeper into debt. There comes a time that you have to stop kidding yourself and understand that it's over. Admit you messed up, take responsibility, and be done with it. You don't need to bankrupt your family's financial future forever because you're unwilling to give up on a dream that has become a nightmare. It's okay to quit after you've tried everything and it still didn't work. There's no shame in quitting when you've given it your all.

Is that a negative note to end on? You might consider it so, but I don't. Your business is your business and your life is your life. Don't destroy your life because your business didn't work. I have been there. I have had a business fail. I went through every emotion and considered myself a personal failure. But I wasn't a failure. I just failed at that business. I broke most of the rules I laid out here in this book, and I'm not surprised in the least that I didn't make it. I didn't deserve to make it. But looking back, the rule that I broke that hurt me the most was that I didn't quit sooner. I sacrificed too much personally in order to "keep the dream alive." I didn't understand that there was my business, and then there was me. I was worth more than the business ever would be.

As a result of that business failure and the lessons learned, you are reading this book. Thank you for that. I have many others, give them a look!

10

Larry's Ten-Ten-Ten

It only seems appropriate that I should end the book and Chapter Ten with Larry's Ten-Ten-Ten. These short lists will serve you well in both business and in life.

Larry's Ten Rules for Business Success

1. Do what you said you would do, when you said you would do it, the way you said you would do it.
2. A deal is a deal.
3. Do the right thing every time. Not the cheap thing. Not the easy thing. Not the most convenient thing. Just the right thing.
4. Be the person others can count on to get things done.
5. Work hard on your job and work harder on yourself.
6. Never tolerate poor performance in yourself or others.

7. Focus on accomplishment, not activity.
8. Work faster, smarter, and harder.
9. You are paid to work. You are not paid to play, socialize, be happy or love what you do.
10. Manage priorities, not time.

Ten Qualities That Will Never Fail You

1. Honesty.
2. Integrity.
3. Hard work.
4. Being nice to people.
5. Being excellent at what you do.
6. Exceeding expectations.
7. Spending less than you earn.
8. Saving as much as you possibly can.
9. Being charitable with your time, energy, and money.
10. Having a sense of humor.

Ten Steps To A Happier Life

1. Lighten up! Don't get your panties in a wad over every little thing that happens.
2. Forget blame. You can either fix the blame or you can fix the problem. Put your efforts into fixing the problem.

3. Forget guilt. Guilt serves little purpose. If you mess up, apologize and move on.

4. Forget luck. Lucky people are those who are most prepared, recognize opportunities, and take action.

5. Give up the constant need to be right. Pick your battles. Sometimes it isn't worth the fight. Besides, sometimes, you are wrong.

6. Scope up. Pettiness is unattractive on all levels.

7. Rise above the approval of others. You are never going to make everyone happy anyway, so stop trying.

8. Forgive. You can't be happy when you are full of anger and resentment. Get over it. Forgive others for your own sake, not theirs.

9. Get healthy and stay that way. It's hard to be happy and sick at the same time. And success without health isn't really success at all.

10. Stop looking for things outside yourself to make you happy. Happiness comes from within. (Except when you have a bulldog!)

Why It All Matters

In a recent interview, I was asked about my legacy. The interviewer said, "Larry, you've written six *New York Times* and *Wall Street Journal* best sellers, you've spoken to over 400 of the Fortune 500 companies, you're on national television every week, you've had your own television show, you're in the Speaker Hall of Fame and been named one of the Top 50 Keynote Speakers In The World. What a legacy you're going to leave!"

I said to him, "That is not my legacy. All of these accomplishments are temporary and will all soon be forgotten. None are lasting. My legacy is the influence I have had on the lives of my children and the influence they will have on the lives of their children and so on down the line. The influence on the way my lineage will live their lives is my legacy because it is what will last."

What you and I do in terms of accomplishments or making a lot of money doesn't really matter much in the long run. It will be the influence you have on others, and that they in turn will have, that matters most and that will last forever.

We don't change the world, because the world doesn't want to be changed. We change ourselves by becoming better people. If I do that, you do that, and enough individuals do that, then eventually the world will change for the better.

I believe that the role of each of us is to help others to be better people. Because better people do better work. Better people manage their money better, better people serve other people better through their businesses and through their own efforts. Better people raise better kids, and better kids grow up to be better parents. To me, that's what a legacy really is.

That is what this book is ultimately about. This book was written to help you run a better business that serves people by solving their problems. That's a high calling and a worthy goal. And by doing that you will have employees and customers exposed to your values. Your values always show up in the way you deal with others. If your values, your life, and your business influences others to be better in their values, their lives, and in their business, then it's been worthwhile.

CPSIA information can be obtained
at www.ICGtesting.com
Printed in the USA
JSHW051350080621
15682JS00001B/1